CITADEL

ON THE

MOUNTAIN

CITADEL
ON THE
MOUNTAIN

RICHARD WERTIME

FARRAR, STRAUS AND GIROUX · NEW YORK

Farrar, Straus and Giroux
19 Union Square West, New York 10003

Copyright © 2000 by Richard Wertime
Distributed in Canada by Douglas & McIntyre Ltd.
Printed in the United States of America
Designed by Debbie Glasserman
First edition, 2000

Library of Congress Cataloging-in-Publication Data

Wertime, Richard.
    Citadel on the mountain / Richard Wertime. — 1st ed.
      p. cm.
    ISBN 0-374-12378-0 (acid-free paper)
      1. Wertime, Theodore A.   2. Wertime, Richard—Family.
    3. Intelligence officers—United States—Biography.   4. English
    teachers—United States—Biography.   5. Fathers and sons—
    United States.   6. Bunkers (Fortification)—Allegheny
    Mountains.   7. Cold War.   8. Allegheny Mountains—
    Biography.   I. Title.

✓ CT275.W3885 A3 2000
    974.8'7043'0922—dc21
    [B]   00-026892
Portions of this book initially appeared, in somewhat different form, in
two journals. Excerpts entitled "Fowl," "My Father's Death," and
"Presbyterian Ministrations" were published in *Northeast Corridor*,
Volume 3 (1995), pp. 50–61. A longer version of one of the chapters was
published under the title "Echo: *Iran, 1961*," in *Grand Tour: The Journal
of Travel Literature*, Fall/Winter 1997–1998, pp. 131–147.

   I must acknowledge the receipt of a sabbatical leave as well as several
Faculty Development Grants from my employer, Beaver College, which
helped me write this book. Joan and John Jakobson funded the Jakobson
Scholarship that enabled me to attend the Wesleyan Writers Conference in the summer of 1996. I am grateful for the encouragement and
support I received at that conference.

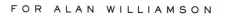

FOR ALAN WILLIAMSON

"... that wretched house of your father's ..."

—Phil Jones, of the CIA, years later

CITADEL
ON THE
MOUNTAIN

My early life divided between two distinct landscapes. One was suburban, crowded, political: Arlington, Virginia, a zone of fast growth and government influence, especially in the community—South Fairlington—where we lived. Part of the largest planned community in the nation (its other half, North Fairlington, lay across a deep ravine that carried Shirley Highway northward), it hosted a sea of buildings, red-brick, neocolonial, constructed to house the burgeoning postwar federal workforce. Children abounded; we were, after all, in the mid- to late 1940s, the very first baby boomers. Everybody's father either worked for the government or was in the military. One of my friends' fathers was the head of the Secret Service; others were five-star generals, or Treasury officials, or higher-ups in the Justice Department; and many of these fathers did work about which we knew absolutely nothing because it was so classified. The Cold War colored the world I grew up in as surely as the Depression did the world of my parents, the world of their parents. The Pentagon—"ground zero"—lay just out of view beyond a hill three miles from us, and it struck me as an absurdity when later, in high school, we were herded into the basement during air-raid drills, made to crouch against a wall, and instructed to pull our sweaters or jackets over our heads. All of us knew—there were 3,200 of us; Wakefield High was huge—that the spot where we crouched would be transformed into vapor within a single millisecond if the H-bomb was dropped.

The secrecy under which so many fathers worked touched my family, too. While traveling through Pakistan a generation later, in the early 1970s, my youngest brother, Charlie, came upon a volume in a bookstore in Lahore; printed in English and published (Charlie noticed) in mainland China, it bore the title *Who's Who in the American CIA*. In the "W"s he found an entry for Theodore Allen Wertime, including a synopsis of my father's career and a brief description of our family.

Accurate—or not? Disturbingly, my mother rests uncertain on the issue. Recently she asked me, "Do *you* think your father ever worked for the CIA, Dick?" On earlier occasions she'd rejected the notion outright; now misgivings have crept in. Maybe she believes that my writing this book has somehow led me to fresh information, since I've conducted a number of interviews with old OSS, State Department, foreign service, and CIA hands. I've reminded her that I'm writing not a history but a memoir.

Besides, my inquiries have yielded no definitive answer. Near the close of his career, my father accepted a pair of foreign service posts: as cultural attaché to the U.S. embassy in Tehran in the early 1960s, when the Shah was in power, and as cultural attaché once again in Athens in the late '60s and early '70s, when the junta ruled Greece. Was the CIA directing his activities then? There are those who think so and would cite as confirmation the fact that after his departure from Athens, when democratic government had been restored in Greece, the staff of the U.S. embassy was given strict orders not to mention his name, ever. Others are casually dismissive of the notion. "Oh, hell," says Joe Yager, my father's old boss in the OSS and State Department, "all of us who served in the OSS during World War Two are thought to have been lifelong CIA agents!"

The fact remains that over the course of a forty-year marriage my mother was in the dark about most of my father's missions, and never even learned where he had trained for the OSS.

The other landscape of my boyhood was as mountainous and rural as the first was suburban. Only a few miles north of the Mason-Dixon line in south central Pennsylvania, it encompassed the Franklin County seat of Chambersburg and the valleys and mountains that lie to its west. These mountains, part of the broad Allegheny sweep, resemble an ocean suddenly frozen into stone; wave upon wave of parallel ridges are arrayed in a march from northeast to southwest. Ironically, the rocks to be found in these mountains—the sandstones and shales, the iron ores and limestones—are constructed from the weathered residues of much vaster mountains that began to lift Alp-like, or even Himalaya-like, along the continent's eastern margins at the end of the Ordovician, some 440 million years ago. These older, higher mountains took shape only gradually over 200 million years. As they slowly eroded, streams carried westward their mud and stone debris, creating deposits that hardened into layered rocks. These strata began to fold between 270 and 260 million years ago, leaving us with the mountains we know today as the Alleghenies. In southern Pennsylvania, in the state's middle section, this even march of waves creates a series of valleys sheltering farms and small towns. The mountains themselves are a deep green in summer, whalelike almost, showing their backs above the valleys; they are sometimes forbidding. The off-seasons mute them, diminishing the pitch of their hues to grays and browns.

In these mountains, human history has been irregular, intermittent. The Buchanan State Forest now embraces much of the region—seventy thousand acres of protected deep woodland through which herds of deer, bears, and wild turkeys roam. In some places, poachers will shoot up the road signs, but otherwise people do little to dent the vast silence of the forests. Unless you step on a stick, or catch a hawk's high cry, or come upon a stream, the low moan of wind may be as much as you hear during a thirty-mile hike.

Yet this region was full of life at the time of this nation's industrial beginnings. Ores from the mountains were carted down into the valleys to be smelted into iron; trees were felled for charcoal, streams diverted and channeled to create millraces. Westward-pushing colonists fought fiercely with the Indians, who under the valiant leadership of brilliant chiefs like Pontiac sought to save their lands. The young George Washington, surveyor and head of the Virginia Militia, served the British general John Forbes as he pushed a road west from Carlisle to Pittsburgh.

The region dropped back, then, into forest, into silence. Some of the valleys were so wild that, in the 1930s, the government sold off land at a dollar an acre to encourage ownership. Woodsmen set their stills deep enough in the forests that no one ever troubled them. Then the lumber companies came and the logging began, but the landscape fought back, thwarting men and their tractors with mud, snow, ravines. Even now, no roads can penetrate in some places.

The Cumberland Valley opens wide to the south here, where the Alleghenies ebb. It runs, with interruptions, all the way to Tennessee. Its limestone is visible as outcrops in pastures farther south than Virginia, but the sedimentary layers express themselves most in shales. To the west, the mountains yield to the Western Reserve, which plateaus away toward the flatlands of Ohio.

Fort Loudon sits at the foot of the Alleghenies where the Cumberland Valley opens; a sleepy town, now, of barely two hundred, it was a major frontier outpost during the French and Indian War. Heading west, the Lincoln Highway bypasses it now as it climbs Tuscarora, one of the highest mountains around. Seven miles to the north lies Cowans Gap State Park, whose cold lake was built by the CCC boys under Roosevelt's New Deal. Franklin County ends at the top of Tuscarora, where Fulton County starts. The view from this mountaintop drops west into the valley that holds the town of McConnellsburg, whose population numbers less than twelve hundred.

Chambersburg. Fort Loudon. Cowans Gap. McConnellsburg. These four locales play a central part in my story. Near Fort Loudon lies "the mountain place," a 66-acre enclave on the side of Hogback Mountain several miles from Cowans Gap that our whole clan purchased in the early 1950s. Here we took vacations and convened for reunions and skated during cold snaps, all of the individual families mixed and jumbled together; eventually, I was one of twenty-four grandchildren. In my earliest memories, we're living in Chambersburg, in a rough, poor section on the other side of the tracks known as Cardboard Village because our barracks-like dwellings—"tempos" built to house ill-paid service families—were so wretchedly constructed. We stayed here, John, Steve, my mother, and I, while my father was in the Army and for the first nine months of his State Department employment, until December of '46. Then we moved to Fairlington, where my last brother, Charlie, was born in 1952.

Chambersburg was my father's hometown. On its easternmost edge, right on the rim of farm country, stood Grandma Wertime's home, a big white house surrounded by gardens and backed by a barn and a large chicken coop. This was the very center of our family, our clan. My father was second youngest of a half dozen children, three boys, three girls: Rudy, Kay, Clara, Selma, my father, and finally Joe.

My grandfather died the winter before the Crash, in a February cold snap. Professor of Music at Wilson College, a very talented pianist who was a strict disciplinarian and a profoundly frugal German, he was taken by pneumonia in three short days. I'd always understood that he had been shaving by an open window. He did die of a chill, but lately Aunt Kay has set me straight on the story: Granddad was accompanying a friend to Caledonia in an unheated car to see a reservoir dam that had just been completed. Apparently this dam was thought a marvel of engineering. On this particular Sunday, which fell, as it happened, during an unusually bitter cold snap, a throng of cars had lined up to get a first glimpse of it. The car had a heater, but it was broken at the time. They'd had to wait for hours because the road was so narrow. By the time they got home, Granddad was ill and declined very quickly. My father was nine.

McConnellsburg enters the story only later. When I was young, it was nothing more than the site of the Fulton County Fair, whose carnival lights and Ferris wheel beckoned in the distance as we crested Tuscarora on hot August nights. It had no real importance until my father decided, in the mid-1970s, to build a peculiar house overlooking the town, on the top of a low mountain named Little Scrub Ridge.

This is the citadel where so many strange things happened.

ONE

A STUDENT OF CHINA

I am six years old and my father is eating breakfast. He hunches at the table in our sparse dining room, his biceps fleshy beneath the sleeves of his T-shirt. The meat at the base of his thick neck folds redly. He is reading the newspaper. Now and then his spoon, wandering forward on its own, takes a stab into his corn-flakes, which are sprinkled with wheat germ. When he has finished eating breakfast, he will dress, walk the hundred yards to the curb of South Stafford, catch the bus into Washington. He'll get off at the terminal at 12th and Pennsylvania and walk to his State Department building on 23rd Street.

He's an expert on China—a "China observer." It's one of the reasons why he reads the morning paper. He's always busy prowling, I am told, for news about it.

He says to my mother, gruffly, "Have you set out my suit yet?"

"Which one?" she asks.

"The herringbone," he answers. His eyes remain glued to some story in the *Post*. "And transfer my things."

"What tie do you want?"

His head lifts. He glares at her. "For Christ's sake, Peg! I don't really care!" His gaze dives back down into the grottoes of the *Post*. "Just make sure that it matches my shirt."

The things to be transferred: Watch. Wallet. Loose change. His spool of dental floss. Keys. A fresh handkerchief that my mother has ironed.

Breakfast is over. My father lifts himself. He marches up to the bathroom to brush and floss his teeth, and to administer olive oil to his dark, straight hair, which he keeps well cut. He favors olive oil on the grounds that it keeps your scalp loose; you should also wrinkle your brow on a regular basis to keep your scalp from getting tight. Tightness of scalp promotes early hair loss. He brushes his hair with ruthless vigor.

"Is my suit out?" he calls.

My parents' bedroom is on the ground floor of our apartment, at the greatest possible distance from the bathroom upstairs. My mother is in their bedroom, or else in the kitchen, busy fixing us breakfast.

"*Peg!*" my father bellows. "*Have you put out my suit yet?*"

"Yes," she calls out wearily.

"Have you transferred my things?"

Again she calls out: "Yes!"

In the same loud voice: "Get out my brown shoes!"

"What?"

"*My brown shoes!* Get them out! Goddammit, can't you *hear*?"

My mother appears at the bottom of the stairs, dish towel in hand. "Ted, I'm busy," she explains. "The boys must eat breakfast."

"*I'M GOING TO BE LATE!*" he screams down at her.

"Your things are all out."

A roll of thunder down the stairs. A furious scrabbling in their bedroom. My father, at last, appears, neatly dressed, elegant, handsome. His hair is slicked back and his shoes are well polished.

"My briefcase? Where's my briefcase?"

"Here." My mother is standing by the front door with his briefcase. She wears a stiff expression.

"All right," says my father. "Good! Now: Tie my tie!"

He gazes into the distance, the line of his jaw tight. His back is straight, his arms militarily rigid at his sides. He looks like a cross between a thoroughly spoiled child and a ferocious drill sergeant.

My mother throws a four-in-hand: the broad part of the tie around the narrow part. Around; under; up; through. Down. She tightens and straightens.

The whole times she is doing this, my father is criticizing. "That's too tight. Loosen a little. I'm going to be late. I wish the hell you'd get my stuff ready for me sooner. Are my dispatches in my briefcase?" It goes on and on.

The tie, at last, is finished. My father grabs his briefcase and his raincoat. "Is there money in my wallet?"

"Yes," my mother answers. "A five and five ones."

He kisses my mother quickly, saying nothing to me or my brothers. He slams out the door, joining the stream of other fathers who flow downtown to be absorbed by the government offices.

"You have to understand! Cruelty means absolutely nothing in China . . ."

The Fairlington Theatre! The Saturday matinee! When the house lights dim and the great velvet curtains swing open with a rustle, it feels as if I'm falling into a pleasant, wakeful dream-space, chuting down the Warner Brothers music that always starts the afternoon.

The newsreel today begins with footage of an air show. B-29s crowd the sky in formation, propellers in a roar, the planes as

neatly spaced against the backdrop of clouds as checkers on a board. The camera cuts abruptly to the throng of spectators, where a pigtailed girl and her stupidly hatted mother are waving patriotic pennants as the planes swarm over. The girl and her mother are smiling. Their free hands are raised to shield their eyes from the sun.

The context alters, transporting us to China. The announcer's voice, so commanding and mellow, is intoning matter-of-factly about mass executions that are under way in Peking. Men are being led out one after another in rapid succession into the center of a huge square. Each has his hands tightly tied behind his back and wears a loose, baggy shift that looks like pajamas. A small paper target with a bull's-eye in its middle has been fastened to the back of each victim's neck. Without ceremony, each of these men is driven to his knees and dispatched with a bullet at the base of the head.

Wave upon wave of men is hurried forth and shot. The city square has filled with their ungainly corpses.

I am gripped by an iron first. Not only the executions but the sheer numbers awe me. How could anybody—? It stuns me even more that these men die unprotesting. Die resigned, wholly silent. *Why aren't they fighting?* As their bodies fall forward, their broad, impassive faces smash hard against the bricks, and their legs jerk briefly. Nothing more to it. For the uniformed guards who are executing them, the work is routine.

I feel caged, suddenly: straps have been fastened across my chest and firmly tightened. I want to look away, but can't. I grope for breath. My bowels go loose. Again I hear the announcer: *"In a purge of the landlords,"* he intones, *"the Communist leaders . . ."*

Numbness settles on me; I scarcely even notice Tom Mix and his cronies fighting off the bad guys and vanquishing the Indians. My father's words return to me: *"You have to understand! Though Chinese civilization is ancient, cruelty means absolutely nothing in China; human life is worthless. They shit in the streets there. They eat dogs, you know; to tenderize the meat, they hang the critters up in trees and beat them to death. With a stick. Yes. A stick. The first time I saw it, it was very hard to watch. But you get used to it. You can get used to anything."*

I step out of the theater into the afternoon sunlight. It's July 1950. My eyes blink and water as they struggle to adjust. Objects seem magnified; the swish-and-rustle of passing cars sounds extra-loud. My hands won't stop shaking. I climb onto my bike to wobble the half mile home.

When I get there, our place is empty. Jesus. Where *is* everybody? I hear my father's words again: *"They shit in the streets there . . . But you get used to it. You can get used to anything."*

I'm not sure *I* can. I cast about our apartment for immediate comfort. Eventually I'm led to the big corner cupboard that dominates our dining room. It's an old maple piece that my father has refinished. He'd brought back with him, from his second trip to China just six months ago, a Chinese silver tea set that is kept in this cupboard. Scenes of life in China decorate all its pieces—the teapot, the coffeepot, the creamer, the sugar bowl. I lift out the teapot. The scenes on it show people laboring in paddies, or pulling heavy wagons up trails in steep mountains, or fishing in fast rivers with bamboo fishing rods. Everything is delicate. Peaceful. Harmonious. The people wear clothes that look like Japanese kimonos, intricate, embroidered. The women have their hair tightly pulled back in buns. Everybody smiles. Then how—?

I put the teapot back and step out the front door, into the long summer twilight. Where the heck is my family?

"They shit in the streets there . . ."

Recently, the Joneses—Ed and Phil—have stopped by. Brothers, sons of Protestant missionaries, they grew up in China and speak fluent Chinese. Ed's a colleague of my father's in the China Branch, at State. Phil is an agent for the CIA. Former OSS members, just like my father, they'd been with him out in Kunming, China, at the close of the war.

I've come into the room while Ed is saying to my father, "So. What do you think?"

The three men fall silent.

"Dick!" my father says. He nods his head only slightly.

Russia has been mentioned, Russia and China, and a new place, North Korea. It's always this way: their voices drop to a murmur in the midst of what appears to be a casual get-together. They are waiting for us—their kids, their wives—to leave the room.

So they can talk.

At night, when the planes fly over, I am lifted from my sleep. We live beneath the flight path into Washington National Airport, just five miles away. The part of Fairlington we live in sits high on a hill looking out toward the Pentagon, and beyond that the city. The roar of the big planes on these humid summer nights shakes and rattles our apartment and jerks me upright on my mattress. *Is it—? Has it begun—?* Hot sweat pours from me. My mouth is chalk-dry.

I live around people who know too much.

LITTLE BASTARDS

He's handsome. Lean. Hard-eyed. His eyes seem even more dangerous than my father's eyes, though they're blue like my father's. Smooth razor jaw. Ears flattened back against his well-shaped skull. Brown hair, neatly trimmed, though a small lock of it falls forward on his brow.

John Churchill: my father's very best war buddy. Here to visit us in Fairlington. He'll spend the night.

It's 1951; I'm nine years old.

He calls us "the little bastards"—John, Steve, and me. Though he means it to be humorous, the phrase sounds steel-edged. Whenever he looks at us, he seems to be peering through our skins and into our bones. He and my father were in India together, in the OSS, before my father flew to China. I've seen pictures of them. Both wear mustaches, .45s on their hips, their uniforms taut over hard-packed muscle. Neither is smiling. In the background is some sort of Indian temple rising like a bad dream, encrusted with statues.

My mother is nervous around John Churchill. She laughs a lot. Smiles tightly. He has brought along with him a shiny German Luger, a pistol made for killing.

Churchill, my father, and my mother go out shooting; in their marksmanship, both men ranked as experts in the Army. The three of them hike across Route 7 into the sandy pine barrens beyond the Episcopal Academy and the adjacent seminary. The pine barrens yield to an oak-and-pine forest if you keep going south, which we sometimes do on foot or by bike; if you kept going farther, you'd be in unbroken forest all the way to Occoquan.

When they return, my mother's quiet. Churchill is sardonic about the adventure; he teases her for having been inept and fearful—they'd set discarded bottles on a pine stump in a clearing; the recoil from the Luger had made my mother's arm jump—and for having hit nothing. When we boys ask to have another look at the pistol, he takes it from its case but tells us flatly, "Don't touch."

John Churchill's a mountain climber. With his fiancée, Nancy, a trim, pretty blonde who kissed my brother John on the cheek once and made him blush deeply, he's about to fly to Switzerland to climb in the Alps. They both love to climb: they're confident people, lean and tanned.

Tonight John Churchill is sleeping in my room, which normally Steve and I share. It's the big bedroom upstairs, with our twin beds facing away from the back wall like rowboats drawn up on either side of a narrow dock. Steve will sleep with my brother John.

Bedtime; I fidget. I lie on my back looking up at the ceiling, wishing for the night-light that we usually keep on—a lamp in the corner with a steep-sided shade. Night still swarms with the dark, familiar figures that trouble my sleeping, and it frightens me to have so large a stranger in the room, someone who makes my mother laugh in that way, and whose looks seem to send steel rods hurtling toward me. The Luger must be resting right there in his suitcase, the shells next to it, each of them a small, deadly, gleaming torpedo.

Am I making tiny noises? I must be, but I'm not aware of it. A curt comment comes from our guest in the dark. His words make me whimper. A rustling occurs, and the next thing I know, my face has ignited. He has risen and slapped me, a quick darting move made entirely in the dark. "Shut up, you little bastard," he says, less in anger than in calm irritation.

By my age, I'm no stranger to the hard hand of a father (my brothers and I will endure ferocious beatings), but this quick explosion has come out of nowhere. I'm left completely breathless. I'm so reluctant now to make any sort of sound that I work to pull my sorrow inside my body. My arms are rigid. My Adam's apple wobbles, and tears sting my eyes. I'd call for my mother, but I know that I won't say anything to her—to her or my father—when tomorrow's light comes. I achieve a pure silence. Night wears away.

The news, months later, that John and Nancy have been killed while climbing in the Alps opens fresh feelings in me. An avalanche has buried them under tons of ice and snow. Their broken bodies, recovered, have been put to rest together.

My father walks around for days with deep furrows etched on the sides of his face. My mother is careful with him—careful, and cautious.

STEEL-MILL SONG

"Jay! Let's hear your song!" one of the grown-ups calls while the other grown-ups smile.

Straight-faced and sober, my cousin Jay goes to the organ. It's a foot-powered instrument, antique and decrepit, with two wheezing pedals and a row of lacquered stops bearing dark Gothic letters. Jay pushes in and pulls out these stops as he eases into play, undeterred by the German words, undeterred by anything. As he will tell you in detail, his song evokes the roar of the Bessemer converter, the huge ladles steaming with fresh molten steel, the hum of shop fans, the grind of cooled girders. He knows of what he speaks: his father, Uncle Joe, is a steelworker employed at T. B. Woods in Chambersburg. We're hearing Jay's "Steel-Mill Song," also known as his "Foundry Song."

My cousin is unusual in everything his mind touches. Ill as an infant, he's regarded as special for the dark oval birthmark he carries over his rib cage, the defect in his hearing, and an energy unmatched in all us other grandchildren.

Strange sounds breathe into the room as Jay's fingers nimbly walk the yellowed keyboard, whose ivory keys are cracked and shivered, like thin ice freshly stepped on. Jay's shoulders hunch forward, his elbows extending in the dim light of the parlor like skinny outriggers holding up a fragile craft; his hair is so dark that he seems, at first glance, headless, and his ethereal music navigates the keys with its own unerring logic. At moments it is concussive; thunderous; monumental. Abruptly it flows into meditative channels where soft trills mingle with a pedal point that hums in some subterranean cavern.

I'm impressed by Jay's performance, which is never twice the same. At school I take piano, and practice—*have* to practice— on our new home upright. The only tunes *I'm* any good at are "Turkey in the Straw" and listless carols like "Silent Night," which differ not a note from one performance to the next.

Eccentric and quarrelsome though we may be, we're a musical family. I play piano; John plays piano; Steve will begin the piano next year, in the first grade. My mother is a pianist who plays with great proficiency, and my father is a serious violinist and violist. Every one of my cousins plays some instrument or other, and I've no aunt or uncle who can't sit down and turn out a melody by Chopin or Brahms. Uncle Rudy's new wife, Aunt P.J., is a splendid opera singer; and Aunt Selma's husband, Jim, is a respected violinist and musicologist. When my grandmother got very angry at my father as a boy—was abnormally vexed at him—she'd take away from him his beloved violin. Mrs. Galtz, in Chambersburg, gave him lessons for free because he had so much passion; because, after the Crash, they couldn't afford to pay.

When he comes home from work, after he's had some exercise, my father tunes up his violin or viola before turning his attention to his scholarly pursuits (he's studying the history of early metallurgy). He always starts his violin practice by playing the same wretched scales every night; then he settles into working on some trio or quartet. Occasionally he'll play a sonata with my mother (scolding her frequently for not keeping tempo), but more often he's readying for his string quartet. Two or three times a month, the group meets in our living room. We tiptoe around then, diffident and quiet once the musicians have arrived; my father is stern with us, just as he is with the musicians. Some are friends, some colleagues. He's the boss. No nonsense here! When the preliminaries are over, the music swells, flooding the room, the sonorities impressive in so modest a space.

There's no home in the Wertime clan where we can't make music. Joe and Vee live now just a mile from Fort Loudon, in an old stone house that dates back to 1734—the year of Daniel Boone's birth. It has a huge open hearth and hand-hewn beams, and a phone activated by an old-fashioned hand crank. We're held here together, Joe and Vee's family and ours, by a gigantic snowstorm on the eve of the 1950s. Over the course of the three days that the blizzard is raging, we enjoy many performances of Jay's "Steel-Mill Song." We all take turns at the old wheezing organ.

Grandma Wertime's living room harbors *two* pianos, a battered old upright with loose key action and a stiffer-keyed baby grand, a Mason & Hamlin. When my aunts and uncles were younger, the upright resided in a bedroom on the second floor. If two of the children wanted to play a piece for four hands, a third child would be stationed on the stairs halfway up to conduct the performance. The Mason & Hamlin is the instrument my grandfather practiced so hard on for his upcoming recitals. A formal portrait of him sits on top of it. I'm always struck by the fact that he has a dimpled chin, just as I do. From this picture it's hard to tell what a temperamental man he was, what a strict disciplinarian. He once whipped Aunt Selma so hard with his belt that her vision was badly impaired for several days.

We're frequent visitors to Grandma Wertime's place. Until we buy a car at the end of the 1940s, we travel there by Greyhound; and even after the mountain place is acquired in the early '50s (in part because we've grown to be so many in the family), my father sees to it that we visit his mother often. He can't not fight with her—they have arguments that sometimes wear on for hours—but we go nonetheless.

It's August, late 1940s. I gaze out from the back porch of Grandma Wertime's place. Her high wild peach tree is heavy with mottled fruit. Too near the house to suit anybody's pleasure, this tree is old, its peaches dingy; they drop on the pavement, bringing bees and yellow jackets. The bees migrate here from the Freshauers' hives, those ominous white boxes that sit behind their house on a fenced-in plot that Mr. F. never enters unless he's wearing his bee suit. The peach tree will fall to the axe by the time I am seven; in its place will be planted a thorny blue spruce that might as well be a cactus.

Bees, yellow jackets. They're among the things I fear here. So are the spiders. Especially in the outhouse: they cast their wide nets, their unholy cornucopias, in all of the corners and on both windowsills. They lurk in their funnels, their brown legs grizzled and their backs brutally hunched. Moving or motionless, they make my spine shiver. I must utilize the outhouse because my father insists on it; we haven't any need, he says, to use the regular bathrooms (there are two here, full ones, with white porcelain bathtubs and clean, spiderless toilets) when there's a perfectly good shanty right there, in the backyard. Besides, it conserves water. Water here is precious. My grandmother's water comes from rain on her roof. It runs down through screens into a large concrete cistern beneath the floor of the laundry room, a dark, ringing cavern through whose trapdoor my father drops once in a while to make repairs. I find it strange that such a volume of dark, cold water lives beneath the wooden floorboards. But a bright red hand pump lifts the water from this cistern up into the scrub tub; it's fresh in the drinking cup that waits there for us.

Browned, dusty piles of rejected *Reader's Digest*s populate the outhouse, whose windows are begrimed with deep, ancient dirt. A small wooden structure, the outhouse is surrounded by a thick ring of spruces that shuts out the sunlight. The only thing visible is the white toilet paper. And the shadows of spiders.

My grandmother's chicken yard also tests my courage. I am famous in the family for having pestered one of the roosters with a long pole shoved through the fence of this coop when I was

only two years old. Someone caught a photo of me right in the act. The pole is so long it's a wonder I can hold it. I'm a complete Nordic blond, just like my older brother.

It has been, perhaps, the taking of the photo that has done it: all the roosters in the yard seem to bear the dark memory of my earlier abuse. I cannot step through the gate without fearing that some sharp-spurred dandy will take exception to my presence and cock a glazed eye at me. I carry a stone or peach pit; whenever a rooster comes at me, wings flapping, beak open, its body up on tiptoe, I let my weapon fly.

Oddly, when my father's there, the roosters never bother me. I go about collecting the eggs from the still-warm straw-lined boxes without any trouble. The straw inside the boxes has been rounded and rendered shiny, like the inside of a bowl; the hens never foul it. I can smell their recent tenure: it's a sweet, musty odor, fully motherly. Trusting.

For all that, the chicken yard is a place full of violence. Skunks and weasels, and an occasional raccoon, creep in here by night to steal eggs; I have watched on autumn evenings when my father and Uncle Joe have staked out the henhouse, the floodlight in my father's hand, the rifle in Joe's. When a skunk comes, the air is filled with the scent of thick brewed coffee overlaid by a fearful musk. My eyes drip tears. Joe and my father talk in whispers; my uncle's gun is steady as the skunk's forked stripe blazes up into the floodlight. The rifle barks; the skunk leaps. "Good shot," my father says.

"Good shot," he repeats. His strong jaw works.

We approach with slow steps to make sure the skunk is dead. Sometimes my uncle pumps several bullets into it just to be certain. I swallow hard watching this; each shot makes the skunk's limp body twitch and skitter.

The chickens twitch, too, when my father cuts their heads off. A squat piece of phone pole serves as executioner's block. It's kept in the barn and set up in the gravel by the barn's wide doors, away from the coop, when it's time for beheading. I'm eight the first time my father gives me the hatchet and invites me to do it. "All right," he advises. "Both hands. Draw it up slowly. You don't want to hurry."

I'm impressed by how different a chicken looks when it's swinging upside down in my father's strong grip. Especially the hens. They make soft, absent noises as they prowl about the chicken yard, pecking and cooing. They're never in a hurry. Their feathers have a soft, glossy, feminine shine to them. They know that death is coming as soon as my father lunges at them; they squawk, trying to skitter away, but he's too quick for them; he catches and swings them over so that their wings fall open. They flail in the air, yawping; and yet, as soon as they're fully mastered, they cease their commotion and let their heads hang down, turning this way and that. They seem curious, attentive.

They behave the same way with their heads on the block, one eye looking at you. Watching the action.

My feet plant in gravel. I grab a quick breath, and the rest is pure pleasure. The hatchet falls hard. It ca-*thunks*, embedding itself in the top of the block. It's hard to tell that there was even a chicken's neck there.

The head falls to the ground. The beak opens mutely. It's as if the chicken wants to share one final thought with me. Its eye blinks twice.

The real fun is elsewhere. "Stand aside!" my father says, and carefully sets the bird down on its two clawed feet. When he releases it, the chicken sprints around us in a circle, its wings flapping wildly while we shout and cheer it on. Blood bolts from its neck. After several seconds of this, it keels sharply over, having lost its last balance. Its legs may scrabble.

It's ready for plucking, the part that I hate and always try to beg off on. My aunt Clara takes a particular relish in doing this. She's a pediatrician—she lives in Lemoyne, near Harrisburg— who enjoys frightening me. She likes to see the look on my face during the plucking, which begins with a kettle of boiling water in the yard; she loves to watch me squirm as she pulls out the crop, the intestines, and other innards. "What's the matter?" she says, grinning. "You don't like that smell?"

I fear giving her an answer: a permanent crease occupies the space between her eyes. It's a crease that gives her brow a kind of ominous, dangerous cast. Her teeth are white and sharp.

Thanksgiving Day, November 1946. Snow sprints at us from its tunnel in a muted sky. We are headed "down the lane," as we always call the journey, to Blaine Hearst's farm to fetch the turkey for dinner. There is quite a crowd of us: my uncle Joe; my cousin Jay, just a few months younger than I am; my brother John, my father, and me. My mother has bundled me into my bulky winter coat and shoved boots on my feet; I am swaddled yet cold. Blaine's farm lies half a mile straight down the lane, a rough graveled road that lifts and dips through the cornfields spreading out on either side. The stubble looks like knives pointing up through the snow.

We've brought along a sled on which to tie the live turkey, a worn Flexible Flyer large enough for four children. Blaine's farm perches above a bend in the creek, the Conococheague, which takes a hard left at the foot of the dark rocks where his lower pasture starts and heads out toward Red Bridge. The farmhouse is brick; a black weathercock stands atop its slate roof. The barn is a vast white structure, rich-smelling and hulking; the foghorns of mooing cattle reach us from a distance. The falling snow welds the house and barn to each other. They form a large ship that cuts a misted channel toward us.

The barking of the dogs starts up as we approach. They are black, leggy curs with short, shiny pelts and a predatory lope. They circle in on us, growling and nipping. Even my father has to shoo them off roughly.

Blaine is a big man, ruddy and pleasant. Hooks instead of buttons fasten his gray collarless coat; the term *Mennonite* hangs in the space above his family like a tall, imposing shadow. His children—he has many—have large hands and faces whose fair skins stretch over broad, untroubled cheekbones. His boys are rough and smiling; they're big kids, accustomed to a farm's raw mysteries. Their names intimidate me: Joel. Jerry. Vernon. We amuse them, it seems; they pay us little mind, though every now and then their eyes give us a furtive flicker.

The turkeys are penned in one corner of the barnyard, behind chicken wire that separates them from the cattle. In order to get to them, we must pass through the barn, an envelope of sudden night, straw-strewn and pungent; large wooden beams reach their clumsy arms toward me and the cows noisily shift their bulky weight in the dimness. We come out of the barn beneath a sheltering overhang; the snow now falls faster. I stand in the lee with my brother and my cousin while the men go into the coop. The bird that they hunt down is huge, a tom turkey; once they capture it, they tie it with a hemp rope and hurry it past us, back outside to the snow-sifted sled. They lash the turkey down. Blaine makes a rough joke that amuses Joe and my father. It impresses me how little animal misery means to Blaine.

Jay and I are ordered to ride with the turkey. I whine, but obey; my toes have gone numb in the tight-fitting boots, my ears are on fire, and my fingers find it difficult to grasp the edge of the sled. I sit huddled forward. Jay is so near me that our coat sleeves rub.

My eyes cannot pry themselves loose from the turkey. Subdued, it does its best to lift and turn its head around. Guided by its hooked beak, its expression fully quizzical, its eye seeks out mine. Its fleshy neck rivets me; it reminds me of the goiters that I sometimes see on older people in Chambersburg. They are usually country people, overweight mostly, with rugged red complexions. The turkey's wattles are uglier; they form a bright tumor, a loose scroll of flesh that seems somehow wrong. The bird's red claws clutch vaguely at the air.

"Okay," my father says at the end of our journey. We've reached the white doors of my grandmother's barn. The bracing snowy outing has put my father in a good mood. "Let's get out the hatchet," he says, "and do old testicle-head, here, justice."

The turkey squawks. My uncle laughs.

So does my father.

TWO

ECHO

June 1961. The outskirts of Tehran fall behind us quickly. My father drives a car he has borrowed from the Agency, a battered Ford wagon we will park on the roadside when the going gets rough. If it's looted, no problem.

We're going into the mountains in search of the Alamut, the fortress made famous in the late eleventh century by the terrorist leader Hasan-e Sabbah. It's deep in the Alborz Mountains, in the Valley of the Assassins. The roads are so bad that Guilanport has armored his VW Beetle with thick steel plates, plates he's had welded to the car's underside. He travels up ahead of us. Our companions ride with him.

First we'll drive to the town of Qazvin; from there we'll sheer off north, into the foothills. We'll all have to fit into Guilanport's Beetle for the final leg of our trek once we've left the Ford behind. Our camping gear is tied to his overloaded rack.

Right now we're doing eighty. This is one of the things about my father in Iran—he loves to go fast. At home, he's always careful, fearful of putting too much wear on his tires.

The newly minted pavement stretches black into the distance; no center lines have been painted on it yet. Pools of hallucinatory water form and vanish. In the early 1960s, a highway of this sort is still a novelty in Iran; the paths that traverse the great central deserts—the Dasht-e Kavir and Dasht-e Lut—are rough gravel washboards that jolt the teeth and kidneys, and silt every pore with grime.

What a stark country this is! The sunlight is searing. The Alborz Mountains bulk up on our right, gigantic heaps of mud at times, at other times glinting like colossal iron pyrites. Oases along the roadside lurk behind mud walls, their palms feathering up into the air like ostrich plumes. The smell of burning dung stabs its gunpowder stench into our eyes and nostrils.

My father starts to tell me about his visit with Ezat Negahban, Iran's top archaeologist. "You recall how hot and muggy the Caspian is," he says.

"Yes," I answer. We'd camped there for two days not three weeks before this, my father and I, with all three of my brothers.

"Well, Ezat was living in this squalid thatched hut—maybe, oh, two hundred yards from the edge of the beach. I'd arrived up there in the late afternoon; there was a breeze coming in, but the temperature was still somewhere up around 100. He gave me a thorough tour of the excavations they were doing. Absolutely incredible stuff! Then I took him out to dinner at one of those wonderful outdoor restaurants overlooking the water. A handful of tables; an open grill; not much else. But what wonderful lamb!

"When we got back to his place, it was right around dusk. Then he did the damnedest thing! He took an enormous glass jar from a shelf and put it right on the table. Then he took this little gadget—it was a kind of cherry picker, with a pull-cord and a sort of bent hook on the end—and pushed it right up into the thatch of his roof. The next thing I knew, he had picked a small snake—just like this!—out of the thatch and dropped it into the jar. Kraits, for the love of God! Then he picked out another. And another. And another."

I've listened intently.

"You understand?" says my father.

"I think so," I say. "Kraits—"

"The 'sixty-second snake.'" My father hasn't waited. "That's what the Persians call them. 'If you're bitten by a krait, find the cool of a shady tree; you'll be dead in sixty seconds.' So I said to Ezat, 'For the love of Jesus, man!' I've never seen a man so calm. And he just shrugged and said, 'Oh, you get used to it.' Whatever Allah wills, you see . . . The jar contained formaldehyde. There must have been twenty dead snakes inside it."

My memory is stirred: *"You can get used to anything . . ."*

My father dips his head, his brief tale concluded. He's been cultural attaché in Iran for less than a year now; it's the first of his overseas foreign service assignments. He's been Deputy Director of Research and Analysis for the USIA since the mid-1950s, when he left the State Department.

He likes being out here in this wild part of the planet. He has forged for himself, with discipline and dedication, a parallel career as a serious historian of ancient technology. The archaeological treasures of this ill-explored land hold a special interest for him quite apart from his work here as cultural attaché. John and I arrived, in Grandma Schultz's company, almost four weeks ago. We both attend Haverford College. I'll be a sophomore, John a junior. Steve and Charlie, my younger brothers, moved out here with my parents a year ago this August. They attend special schools for expatriate children.

I'm still adjusting to this place. Tehran is as high—a full mile above sea level—as Mexico City; it's hot here, brutally arid; and I'm struggling to absorb my first experience of Islam. It hasn't been easy. I've already suffered from a bad bout of sunstroke and the Tehran trots.

But I'm up for this trip. We'll camp for the first night at the head of the valley, whose length we'll have to hike in order to get to the Alamut. My brothers have chosen not to come. The heat, maybe . . . or my father.

The Caspian raises no deadly snakes for us. But we have to cross the Alborz over the feared Chalus Pass, a breathtaking journey in all the worst ways.

"Don't look," my father tells us. But we already have. A thousand feet below us, the car that has plunged lies broken and scattered like an insect freshly stepped on. The bloodstain of fractured glass, of twisted chrome and metal—it's a red car, a convertible—is surrounded by a horde of ants: rescuers or onlookers, milling around aimlessly.

My stomach churns. "I wonder if anybody survived."

"I doubt it," says my father. "It isn't likely from this height."

Just then we come around a sharp hairpin turn and have to swerve ourselves, precariously, to keep from hitting a melon truck that is coming straight at us. It's full to the brim, beyond the brim, with ripe, dark melons; the driver hangs halfway out the window, screaming at us, his horn steadily blaring despite the fact that he's in our lane.

We just squeak by him, our tires feathering lightly on the edge of the abyss.

"Tell me when we get to the Caspian," I mutter. I drop over my head, like a loud, ringing helmet, an old pot of my mother's we've brought along to cook with. I close my eyes resolutely, immune to my brothers' teasing.

The Chalus Pass, from here, falls ten thousand feet in the space of several miles through a series of steep turns so stark and hair-raising that I have no wish to look. But I can feel the car descending. It's been five hours now since we've left Tehran and started the climb over the mountains. We've been grinding over gravel the entire way; my once-white shirt is almost black from the dust.

We strike out for the Alamut at five in the morning, in the company of the guide we arranged for the previous evening. The guide, a local man, wears the tight felt cap and the baggy pajama outfit of an Iranian peasant. His face bears pockmarks and his teeth have thoroughly rotted. We're incredulous when he tells us that the Alamut is twenty-five kilometers in the distance. Guilanport and my father tell him he must be exaggerating.

We've slept by a river, uncomfortable stones beneath our bedrolls. I've shared a tent with my father; our three Iranian companions have shared a larger, fancier tent pitched at a distance from ours. Muffled giggles issued from its precincts last night, leaving me to wonder once again how things stand here.

The connection between Guilanport and my father remains unclear to me; I know that Guilanport is the Shah's ski instructor and a serious Alpine climber. Part French, part Persian, he's a short, affable man with deeply bronzed forearms and a creased, kindly face. The others are a youngish Iranian woman who works for my father at the USIA and her nine-year-old son, Parviz. The woman's name is Leilah. I take it that she's divorced—a rarity, still, in Iran—and that she and Guilanport are probably lovers. What her connection is with my father more exactly I can't say. Parviz, for his part, is an olive-skinned boy with large brown eyes who almost never speaks a word and doesn't know English. But he makes the rugged trip we're undertaking without complaint.

The river we've slept by is a noisy mountain torrent. As we push off on our journey, we enter a chilly canyon whose high walls close around us. The sun disappears and we can see our breath. The river deepens, narrows; our trail dead-ends suddenly. I can't help wondering what we're getting ourselves into.

But our guide reassures us. We are going to have to ford here; I sensibly sit down and take my boots and socks off. My father does likewise, as do Parviz and his mother. After tying the laces together, we sling our boots over our shoulders. Guilanport shrugs while we sit there with our feet bared, his face turned away, and manfully wades into the waist-deep water fully shod. Watching him, I think, *Uh-oh, he'll regret it!*, and it turns out I'm right. By the time our journey's over, his feet will be shredded.

Our guide proves accurate: the round trip to the Alamut is a long, wrenching, often tedious thirty-one miles. We won't make it back to our campsite till after midnight. But once we've forded over, the landscape breaks open, and for the next several hours we slog a straight path running parallel to the riverbank. Poplars thrive; the fields are green. Saw-toothed mountains flank the valley into the distance.

The villages are filthy here, the children malnourished. But the grim scenes are tempered by strangeness and beauty. We cross a wooden bridge that spans a wide torrent at the end of the valley; behold a blind camel endlessly circling, threshing grain; gather plump blackberries from stands of canes along the path; skirt a small stone cistern supposedly built by the Romans; and then climb for two hours in a jolting, painful mule train up into the mountains on narrow, rocky trails that leave no margin for error.

As we're nearing the Alamut, we meet an old man laboring up a steep hill with a burden on his back that looks, at first, like firewood. The plunging ravine that he has just emerged from fairly dizzies my sunburned senses.

Guilanport hails him.

The burden on his back isn't firewood. It's a child, thickly wrapped in cloth and canvas.

We ask him, "Where are you going?"

"To Tehran," he informs us. "This child is sick. My grand-daughter. I am walking to Tehran. To the hospital. She's in fever."

"But Tehran," says Guilanport, "is almost fifty miles away."

"Then I've no time to squander," he answers us, smiling, the gold in his molars taking the afternoon sun.

There is joy in his smiling as we turn and watch him go.

I know about crisis. Everything in this country appears to be in crisis. At the outset of our trip to the Caspian three weeks ago, we'd cautiously had to make our way, on the city's northern rim, through a procession of chanting flagellants some fifteen thousand strong—men wailing mournfully and whipping their bare, blackened backs with lengths of chain. "It's a Muslim holy day," my father turned in the car to tell us. "A day of atonement. Keep all the doors locked, now, and don't focus your eyes too directly on anybody. They consider it sacrilege."

The great leader Mosaddeq—still a hero in Iran—is under village arrest, and important Iranians are up in arms about it. The Shah lives in fear of a Russian invasion, and has troops on the alert along his whole northern border; the U.S. likewise fears Soviet aggression and pumps billions of dollars into the pockets of the Shah to keep him pro-Western. Most of the money—so my father has said to us—lines the Shah's own pocket. Corruption in his family is so deep and widespread that the Shah's own sister controls most of the heroin traffic; she's said to have her emissaries use the corpses of dead babies, their chests hollowed out, to smuggle heroin over the border into Iraq and Afghanistan.

Crisis is endemic to daily life here. Soldiers roam the streets shooting and poisoning wild dogs, whose numbers in Tehran have swollen to more than a hundred thousand. These are the notorious *jube* dogs; cowardly curs by day, they run in packs at night and sometimes kill and eat children. The *jubes* are the concrete troughs along the edges of the streets through which the city's water runs during mornings and evenings. Since Islam forbids the use of still or standing water, the *jubes* provide the public's water supply, and daily we see such sights as a woman bathing her infant several yards downstream from a urinating donkey. By the time this water has reached the southern side of the city, where a hellish waste of brick kilns fouls the air with dense smoke, it is a thick, viscous ink, black and redolent of garbage.

Islam, too, seems in crisis. Young men and women see so little of each other before they get married that it's nothing to see a pair of uniformed men walking hand in hand, their pinkies interlocked, or kissing deeply at street corners. Soldiers seek to prey on the expatriate children at my youngest brother's school, and have to be shooed off.

Even at my parents' house, a diplomat's villa complete with swimming pool in the suburb of Shemiran, where oleander blooms and watered beds of flowers make bright, intricate patterns, crisis abounds. There's of course the daily crisis of my father's conduct: he's irascible and bossy, altogether domineering. A caged bear in the house, he's marginally easier outdoors. He fusses at my mother, swaps harsh words with Grandma Schultz, and keeps us boys on the move. We are helping him, in the evening, read the galleys of his first book, *The Coming of the Age of Steel*. It's a task that I, as a would-be writer, could take pleasure in; but with him it's like swimming in a molten bath.

It's more than just domestic. The gardener Rajab Ali, an elderly man with a twinkling smile, is thought to be acting as a spy for the Shah's police. The house may be bugged; we must often talk in whispers. Thousands of dissidents, the rumor goes, are being tortured, and SAVAK has packed its prisons. Flatterers hedge the Shah about on all sides; what he knows and doesn't know, no one can be entirely certain.

My father's own position doesn't lack ambiguity. He claims (I've no way of knowing what the truth of this is) that he outranks, militarily, even the top brass in Iran because of his status as a congressional appointee, and he, at least, feels that this engenders resentment; his intellectual interests bring suspicions upon him; and while he evidently works for the USIA, whose libraries are targets for terrorist bombings, some people believe that his real employment is a mystery. I'm privy to little, so cloaked in secrecy has been his government career. I'm aware, of course, of the hazardous trip he made to North Korea in the winter of '51, when MacArthur broke the North Korean line at Pyongyang, but understand nothing of his other special missions. That he has worked in intelligence for a great many years under top-security clearance is about all I know. A man who "gets things done," he's seen as tough and decisive.

My brothers and I can vouch for that.

It's four in the afternoon when we reach the Alamut. Here our guide leaves us. In the village that huddles at the foot of the great rock, we stop to have tea at a roadside teahouse—a mud hut, merely, but carpeted inside with rich Persian rugs. A large brass Russian-style samovar bubbles, and the owner is smiling. We drop on the carpets and stretch our weary legs, ignorant of the fact that we're committing an offense: protocol requires that we sit cross-legged. Words exchanged in Persian correct our behavior. We sip Indian tea through lumps of hard sugar that we clench in our teeth.

Refreshed, we're left to assault the last leg of our journey, up the back of the rock. It's difficult and dangerous, the slope very steep and almost sandlike in consistency. Parviz and his mother have declined this final ascent, so it's only my father, Guilanport, and me. I creep, terrified, on my knees and elbows. Even Guilanport, as skilled and practiced as he is, picks his way up with caution. My father, in contrast, fairly scampers on up while I am clutching at rough handholds and cringing at the dropoff.

I pull myself up onto the platform at last, fighting to restore my ragged breath and repair my courage. "*C'est bien évident,*" I say to Guilanport, "*que vous êtes montagnard.*"

"*Oui, j'ai l'honneur d'être montagnard*," he answers. The pride is clear in his voice.

The vista that confronts us is depressing, if awesome—the most desolate and barren set of hills and rugged mountains; no vegetation; the backbone of the planet laid bare to the aching eye. Yet once upon a time a goodly fortress arose here. From this remote site the fabled Assassins sallied forth, drug-crazed, fanatical, determined in their mission—the murder of political leaders inimical to the movement. They would journey to the far ends of the earth to fulfill their mandate. The great Persian poet Omar Khayyám, a friend to the sect that had its stronghold here, may have stood where I'm standing. But it's hard to envision. The top of this rock seems scarcely big enough to accommodate any building, much less a grand fortress and its fabled pleasure garden. Its surface now is littered with bits of tiles and potsherds, most likely debris from the recent encampments of shepherds.

I ask my father to tell me more about the Assassins. The men trained as killers first were given hashish (the English word *assassin*, he adds, comes from the Arabic *hash-shashin*), and then were indulged in every imaginable sensual pleasure. "They were made to feel, you see, that they had entered Paradise—and they wanted to remain there. Brainwashed and addicted, they were ready to do the bidding of the leaders of the movement—or else lose Paradise! Some people claim, you know, that the Assassin movement is alive in Persia even today."

I nod. Something has stirred me. "So, what happened when— who was it, Genghis Khan?—finally overran this place?"

"No," says my father, "Actually it was Hulagu who conquered it, in 1254. Brother of Mangu Khan, the great Mongol Tatar. They were Genghis Khan's grandsons. Hulagu hanged everybody. Down to the last man. The thunder of the hoofs of his cutthroat horsemen filled this whole valley, and the string of his mounted soldiers disappeared into the distance. It must have been quite a sight!" My father draws my attention to a broad, dark seam in the rock fifteen yards below us. "Notice the cistern.

They carved it out of bedrock. They weren't going to be driven out of here for lack of water! It finally took an overwhelming force to defeat them."

My father's eyes glitter. And yet, while he's speaking, I can't help wondering, *And what kinds of terrorism does YOUR agency sponsor—whatever agency it is?* But of course I say nothing. It seems anticlimactic, our having made it up here finally, after so long a journey—and for *what*, exactly?

We start back shortly and are rejoined in the village by Parviz and Leilah. Again the jolting ride over the mountains on the mules, the long, boring hike, the hamlets, the bridges. We go without dinner because we've brought too little food; soon it gets dark, and for the last four hours we hike under moonlight. Parviz and his mother remain quiet and uncomplaining, so I try to be, too. But a headache has wormed its way into my skull. My feet hurt, feel heavy; my mouth is dry—we're out of water; and as we trudge along, I make a promise to myself. *I'm not going to forget this. I'll never let myself forget how miserable I feel now. I won't romanticize this, this trip, this expedition, some decade down the line when I'm dull and forgetful. Lord, is my head pounding!*

Still, the moonlight gleams on the mountain to our right. The sky is clear, no clouds; a cool breeze stirs; the moon hangs full, impossibly big.

And in the sky directly over us, a bright star travels with us as we trudge down the valley. It's *Echo*, the satellite balloon we've put up—we Americans, we achievers. A handful of normal stars scatters out behind it, clear and visible through the moon-light . . . stars that appear to give off a faint murmur.

Echo follows us.

PARENTAL GUIDANCE

If you're married too early—married, say, at nineteen; if you wed a high-school girl you've managed to get pregnant through ignorance and failed communication of the worst sort; if you have that child, a daughter, in impoverished circumstances, having taken up residence in a drafty garage apartment near the college you attend—your wife has quit school, her heart never really having been in her education; if, I say, having done this, you manage to get through your undergraduate years with distinction in your major and make it into graduate school, determined as you are to let nothing stop you from getting your Ph.D.—though, by means of a miscommunication now unnervingly familiar, you manage amid your studies to father a *second* child, a son, even prior to the attainment of your bachelor's degree, so that by the time you're twenty-one you are the parent of two children and partner in an altogether unsuccessful marriage; if, in your unhappiness, you punctuate the beginning of your graduate career with misdeeds involving yet other young women, who also demonstrate their ability to have children (this you learn the hard way, at no minor expense, which you must now bear in secret); and if, further, it emerges, the problems of some of these young women properly seen to, your own misadventures turn out to be mirrored, mirrored and echoed, to your infinite surprise and naive astonishment, by misdeeds of your *wife*—why, then you might be in for a spell of heartache and trouble; you might, for the first time in what suddenly feels like a very short life, seek professional advice, not only in the offices of a very costly lawyer (*Why in hell does everything have to cost so much?*) but also in the precincts of a counseling clinic that does *not* cost so much; you might, in truth, find yourself, crazed by jealousy and grief, yet oddly unremorseful about your own activities, actually stalking your estranged, now monstrous-seeming wife, even to the point of spying on her at night with a pair of field glasses (you have rented yourself a room in an elderly woman's house just a couple of miles away), and perhaps, on one occasion, though you haven't really meant to, smashing in her front door and beating up her naked lover, relieved that your children have slept through the fracas; you may, in sum, after these and other such misadventures, dazed, disoriented, in the grip of confusion and feeling altogether beached, find yourself so splintered that you can't get any sleep and nightmares stalk what little rest you do get.

All this I have done. By age twenty-four.

For the love of holy Jesus.

My father phones in consolation. Since returning from Iran in 1963, he's been editing *The Forum of the Air*, a cultural program for the Voice of America. "Say! Dick!" he says. "We're all driving up to the mountain place this weekend. Why don't you join us?"

I say I'm not sure.

"Oh, come on!" he says. "It'd be *good* for you. We'll have some recreation together—croquet, badminton . . ."

Recreation! Yes. I think of all the times that my parents have sponsored what they think are my interests—think, too, of the many times when my brothers and I have engaged in sports with my father, touch football or tennis or whatever is at hand; he's ferocious, my father, in his need to win, to vanquish. A Thanksgiving Day game can turn as deadly and earnest as a heated Super Bowl, and we can limp back to the house with bruised bones and torn shirts that leave us sullen and silent.

But he keeps up the pressure: "You deserve a break!" he says. "A chance to put things in perspective. I won't say that you shouldn't feel weighed down these days. You've got a lot on your plate." He pauses, just briefly. "Why, you know, we could break out your old fishing rods! Stalk a few bass together. I'll bet that those rods are still up there, in the front loft!"

Within minutes I'm undone. Against my better judgment, I've given in again.

I'll come out, I tell him.

It's around noon when I get there.

As I pull into the lane, a corridor of hemlocks and clean maple saplings that explodes into the open when you get to the lower house, the place tightens about me in an old familiar blend of—what? Excitement, claustrophobia . . . that essence of copperhead, of blacksnake and spider, groundhog and deer, horsefly and yellow jacket. No place on the planet can be more buggy than these acres. Or swampy, or humid.

The heat is up today, pounding into the mid-90s. Late August in the mountains. I've gotten off the Pennsylvania Turnpike at Willow Hill, two interchanges to the west of Carlisle, and taken Route 75 down Path Valley almost to Fort Loudon. My shirttail has flattened to the curve of my sweaty backside during the

hours it has taken me to drive from Philadelphia. A bright, high haze is amplifying the sun.

A flood of memories hits me: the loud summer picnics with the full clan assembled; the ice-skating parties in the middle of winter; all the hateful early work it took to get the place in shape, back in the early 1950s . . .

My father is first to greet me. He issues from the lower house just as my car is banking off into the grass by the old rock pile at the edge of the woods. He's dressed—I see in an instant—in his favorite summer outfit: tattered bathing trunks that hang low on his hips and belly, a filthy white T-shirt, a frayed pair of sneakers that he wears without socks, a grimy old ball cap—the same cap he's worn here every summer since my childhood. You can almost not tell what a handsome man he is, with his fine, molded eyebrows, his good, straight nose, his well-modeled chin. The camouflage is perfect.

Greetings. Firm handshakes. He invites me to come in. I quip that he looks ready for a diplomatic function in his elegant attire, but the joke goes over thinly. It's 1966. My own trip to Iran in the summer of '61 is still fresh in my mind, yet seems a century in the past.

The log house is dim after so much sunlight. Scents of seasoned chestnut, of vanished skunk and mouse dirt, spike the air I step into. It's a rudimentary house that is freighted with limits—jury-rigged lighting, electric cables stapled to the walls and the ceilings; cold running water; an outhouse twenty swampy steps from the back door. This is a place where only certain things can happen, what with the furnishings, old and cast-off, and the out-of-the-way location.

Assembled are my mother; my brothers Steve and Charlie; my uncle Joe; my aunt Vee; my cousin Jay; and a friend of the family I'll call Jen Hodges. Jen, about thirty, is the cellist in my father's current string quartet. It surprises me a little to discover she's here, since my father hadn't mentioned her coming along this weekend, but the surprise doesn't last long; we'd folded Jen into ourselves—the clan *and* the family—a decade ago.

I greet everybody. My mother engulfs me in smiles and red lipstick. My hand goes out to Steve and Charlie; I greet Jay, hug my aunt, banter with Uncle Joe, always happy to see him. Greetings, finally, to Jen.

"Well!" says my father. He's like a Boy Scout leader orchestrating his troops. He suggests that we catch lunch and get outdoors for recreation.

Thrown-together sandwiches and thirty minutes later, we are tromping toward the upper house, the whole group of us abuzz with summer chatter. Badminton and horseshoes are our first station stops. My mother and Vee have remained indoors. Teasing and bad-mouthing, yelling and laughing, the rest of us form teams that vary with the game. Soon we're busy flapping at the dense, misty gnat clouds that gather about our heads, or shooing off horseflies that dive like kamikazes.

I drop into familiar thoughts and warm, deep sensations—the sun on my neck while I dig my bare toes into the gunpowder dirt on the rim of the horseshoe pit; the heft and perfect balance of the horseshoe in my hand; the hot breeze that lifts the summer leaves on the beeches and hickories; the high call of tree frogs and the clatter of cicadas. August is a time of stark white light and deep blue shadows, the moss a dry velvet, the lichen on the boulders curls of tough gray leather.

After horseshoes, badminton. Then down for a swim. The afternoon shadows begin to grow longer. My father catches up with me on the edge of the sand that forms a sloping half-moon beach; the pond spreads behind us, shimmering and green in the afternoon light, its breadth a hall of echoes for the laughter and voices of the others still swimming there. My father says to me, "Let's walk for a bit."

He points his chin to the upper house, a 1930s hunting lodge a hundred yards off at the end of the lane snaking up through the woods. We're both still dripping, our trunks plastered to us. I've pulled on a T-shirt, but my feet are still bare. My father wears his ratty old sneakers and no shirt.

"Sure," I say.

We start walking.

A silence drops between us, like a slice of the deep woods that comes up to the roadside. A thin, leafy silence.

"I've been thinking . . ." he says. I'm familiar with this opener: it's his way of launching into a broad-brush speech on the state of the world or into one of his orations on the changes he thinks we need to undertake as a family. Or maybe this will be one of his sharing-of-wisdom moments. I try to bear with him when this urge comes upon him, since I believe his intentions are essentially good. I know, too, that when he is gripped by this impulse, he loves to hear himself talk.

As our feet crunch the gravel on the road to the upper house, he starts to say something, but I cut in on him.

"It's good to see Joe and Vee. It's been quite a while now."

"Yes," he says absently.

I ask how Jay is doing.

"Oh, the usual," says my father, his eyebrows lifting. "Up to his neck in strange notions."

I chuckle, feeling guilty. "Poor Jay. Well . . . And how's Charlie?"

"Oh, he mopes a good deal. I try to keep him busy. We sent him off to a soccer camp for a couple of weeks this summer."

I pause over this one. After all the lonely time my brother spent in Iran, it's proving tough, I believe, for him to readjust. He'll turn fifteen in February. "Has he made any friends?"

"A few. But not many. The others, as you know, lack your socializing skills."

My father glances at me.

It takes me a second to grasp the reference: my siblings. The whole bunch of them.

I feel a burst of pleasure that I do my best to stifle. "Well, perhaps. That could be."

I decide to change tack. I mention that Jen's being here this weekend surprises me.

"Why, Jen has grown!" says my father. "You remember how diffident, how timid she was when we first got to know her. That pinched Midwestern background."

I say I don't recall.

"Oh, her parents are dreadful people. A pair of narrow-minded bigots from South Dakota. They came east once for a visit; your mother and I hosted them. They didn't have a single kind word for their daughter! You know, they'd taught her not to trust *any* of her basic instincts. They hadn't even wanted her to study the cello! They think music is evil."

Then they must have had a hard time with her sports car! I think, smiling. I recall the many times we'd chummed around with Jen in her flame-red Karmann Ghia after a robust round of doubles—she was a decent tennis player—or after one of our family hikes up along the Potomac. Having felt the lack of sisters, it was fun for me and my brothers to have a woman in our lives we could tease and talk to freely. Chunky and mannish, a somewhat awkward, smiling woman, Jen has always been unassuming and good-natured. And a fine cello player. She's a music teacher for the Fairfax County schools.

Punching through these matters, my father alters his tone. "Dick! I'm glad you're here this weekend. I see that you've come to an important juncture in your life."

"I guess," I say. "I—"

"Let me talk for a minute." His blue eyes level on me. "And let me assure you, I hold your deepest interests *very* much at heart! You took on, courageously, a most substantial burden at a very early age. As someone who—as you know—married fairly young myself and had children quite early, I know what it's like to feel the pressures of adulthood in a precocious sort of way."

This makes me uneasy. "Well," I say, interrupting, "it's not as though I didn't bring the burdens on myself."

"Of course!" says my father. "We all choose our burdens. The question isn't whether we've *chosen* them or not; it's a question of whether we've chosen them knowingly or wisely. I believe that you acted in perfectly good faith in shouldering your burdens! Maybe Jane did, as well. You have, in Kent and Michele"— these are my children—"a fine pair of youngsters who deserve all they can get. And I'm sure that you and Jane are seeking to work things out so that they're properly cared for."

My father takes a pause. I allow him to continue.

"Now, *I* had the war in which to get some growing done, something you've never had. And I'm still glad for that—glad both for my time out in India and China, and glad that *you've* been spared this savage war we're having now. This Vietnam thing is an unholy matter—even though at first, I grant, I thought it had value for the American position from a foreign policy standpoint. Containment could have worked, you know, it just *might* have worked, if Rostow and the others had managed it properly . . . But you'll also remember that I was out in Indochina back in 1955, after the fall of Dien Bien Phu. Yes. With that State Department team. And we filed that report — we were *prophetic*, I tell you! — forewarning the Administration that if we got ourselves involved out there militarily, we'd find ourselves entangled in a fruitless war for twenty years. And the State Department, by God, rejected that report! They couldn't grasp the point that the people of Indochina considered their war to be a war of national sovereignty — *not* a war of aggression and imperial expansion, which is how we thought of it."

My father pauses briefly to squint into the sunlight. He continues without stopping.

"You'll also bear in mind how ferocious I got with the Arlington draft board when they tried to reclassify your brother John 1-A."

"When he took that leave, you mean."

"Yes. That year off from Haverford. It was terrible. Jesus. I had one *hell* of a time with those people at the draft board. They wanted to stick John in an army uniform in the *worst* damn way! They even sent him to New Jersey for a military physical. You remember that. Yes. Well, I wrote to them — wrote them from the embassy, in Tehran! — and let them know, by God, in no uncertain terms, that they weren't going to draft a son of mine for this war! John was coming out to Iran in order to study the Persian language; I would brook no interference with his mastering a language that could well prove vital to the world that we'd live in.

"And they listened. They finally listened! Because, by God, I forced them! The point," says my father, "is that I understood quite well, *and* understand now, that Vietnam is not a war that can help you to grow. World War Two helped *me* grow because I needed to be hardened. I needed that discipline . . . even if so much of it consisted of sheer boredom. You've no idea how much time is wasted in military service—how much time, for instance, you spend standing in line! Christ, you stand in line for everything. Inoculations. Mealtimes. Rifle practice. Jesus, even a chance to sit on the crapper! Why, I read more books while standing in line ... You know, the government issued these cheap paperbacks for troop consumption during the war. Many of them classics. Why, I read everything from Rousseau to *The Federalist Papers!*"

Again my father pauses. "Anyhow. Enough of that. Look. I understand that getting divorced is very painful for you. But I could tell from the outset that your marriage to Jane was destined not to work—just as I knew, I knew in my bones, when you were playing Little League all those many years ago, that you'd never be a hitter. A born fielder—yes! You became a brilliant fielder. But you wouldn't be a hitter, the way John was. *John* was the hitter in the family, with those long arms of his ... And this has been, for you, a marriage that you've needed to escape from."

My father bends forward, his shoulders uplifted in an argumentative hunch that makes his chest slack. My heart is gathering force to offer him an answer, but he rolls right over me. "I could sense," he says, "about Jane, during your final year in high school, that she had too many problems to be free and open with you. That you needed a soulmate who could share your deepest interests and the size of your appetites."

Here his eyebrows lift. "You know, of course," he says, his tone growing familiar, a pause punctuating whatever he's just about to tell me, "that your mother and I have had our problems over the years. In the bedroom, that is. Grandma Schultz poisoned Peg when she was a very young woman. *Poisoned* her! Against sex. The virulent old woman is always there in the bedroom with us, figuratively speaking. So!"—my father pauses, his jaw jutting forward—"I've had to seek my satisfactions, at times, in other quarters."

His face alters suddenly. I find myself entangled in a strange web of feelings and dark confirmations. The next thing I know, he is telling me a story about a pair of prostitutes in a Hong Kong hotel. This would have been, it hits me, during one of his many trips to the Far East on government business. Over the course of my lifetime he's been out to Hong Kong a half dozen times, if not more. At any rate, the prostitutes: He had called the front desk to ask that a woman be sent up ("The Chinese," he informs me, "treat it just like room service"), but when the soft knock came and he opened his door, he discovered that there were *two* whores in the hallway, not just one. The first was a slightly older woman, in her thirties. The other one couldn't have been more than eighteen. They'd exchanged angry words in a blur of Chinese. What happened then took my father by surprise. The younger one lifted the older woman off her feet and threw her— threw her, literally!—across the corridor. Then she barged into his room and slammed and locked the door behind her. "*Across the corridor!*" says my father, for dramatic emphasis. "I have to say," he continues, his face full of amusement, "I was hard-pressed, at first, to perform to my usual standards. Initially, this vigorous young woman proved quite daunting!"

I go blank for a moment. I'm not at all sure how long the moment lasts, but when I hear my father again, he has finished his Hong Kong story and is speaking of other matters. ". . . I could work it, then," he is saying, "so that you and Steve and Jen could be in the back loft together. You wouldn't be bothered! I can guarantee you that. I'll see to your mother."

I offer him a stupid look. My mind has been erased, blotted out, obliterated.

"Jen craves company!" my father urges. "She's a robust young woman! You have no idea how she'd welcome your advances. You know, *she* had a brief bad first marriage, too—to that Robert what's-his-name. An unfortunate one. Yes. You remember well enough! He turned out to be a homo. He cleaned her out entirely when she found out about him. Took every stick she had! She was lucky to keep her car."

My father's face has moved up very close to mine as he is speaking these final words. His jagged lower teeth stand out in the sunlight. He glances over his shoulder as if he wants to be certain that no one can hear us. A full hundred yards separate us from the pond. We're standing here together as still as trees in the mottled sunlight, as invisible as shadows. No one cares what the two of us are saying.

I start to reply, but my mouth is so parched that my words come out cracked. "I just don't think—"

My father interrupts me. "Dick!" he exclaims. Then his voice drops to something between a hiss and a murmur. "Listen. I've felt the goodies!" He repeats: *"I've felt the goodies!"* He pauses for a second. "I can absolutely predict that it's a sure thing with Jen!"

I've begun to slide sideways. I'm just about to fall, so I shuffle both feet in order to square my footing.

"Well!" I say. Words fail me. I look at him numbly.

Our conversation ends. In the seconds that follow, I struggle to take a reading on who and what and where I am. My impulse is to flee—to bolt for my car and race off toward the turnpike. Make my getaway like someone in the old Bible stories, not even glancing back for fear of turning into salt. I can't help wondering how my mother fits in here. As crazy as the extrapolation seems at the moment, the thought occurs to me that maybe she's somehow in league with my father—that both of my parents might be degenerate people hacking away at proper boundaries and rendering other people luckless. I dismiss the idea, though, as unfair to her.

What I do, of course, is nothing. I am held here. Held. The afternoon breeze puts pressure on my back, and the sun bakes my face as I walk down the lane. My best response, now, is to plunge into things. Divert myself.

I'll swim again.

I'm calm by the time I've climbed out of the water. I feel confident for the moment that my father's crazy scheme won't come to fruition—can't possibly be something that I will accede to. I'm not entirely clear what will keep it from occurring, but I know that something is going to happen to prevent it. I smile with well-being as I towel myself off. I'm just twenty-four; my gut is still flat, my body trim and capable.

The woods come into focus. The crowns of the trees are almost olive in the sunlight, which is slanting to the west now, pulling longer, darker shadows from the edge of the deeper forest. It's at this time of evening that we have to be careful of our friends underfoot; the copperheads like to come out at this hour, the day's heat past, to bask on the roadway or hunt in the grasses. We've killed a number of them just at this hour, some of them close to the edge of the pond.

I dress. Suppertime nears. Corn must be husked, the table set, drinks put out. In other families this would be a happy commotion; but my father presides here, barking orders and bossing people. No one objects because it's just our routine.

We are going to be eating at the table on the screened-in porch that faces into the woods. The porch is high enough to feel like a veranda overlooking a greensward. A cluster of yucca plants, dry-looking and tall, with white blooms now, borders the path that leads down to the outhouse, which is partially hidden by the overhanging trees. A big white porcelain cold-water sink occupies the corner of the porch farthest from the table.

I'm in a teasing mood during these preparations. My father goes outside to do "a quick bit of mowing" while the rest of us work on supper. I taunt Jen gaily on this or that issue, much as I did when I was fifteen or sixteen, provoking her familiar, somewhat defenseless laughter. I clown with my aunt, a lovely brown-eyed brunette who still, in her late forties, has a girl's lithe body and faultless white skin. She's wearing a sleeveless blouse and snug khaki shorts.

My mother seems oblivious to any undercurrents. A buxom woman with dyed blond hair, she chats with my uncle while she tends to the fried chicken, happy enough to have my father out mowing. Jay grumps around; Charlie has skulked off. Steve, speaking little, helps me get the table set.

We eat. The meal finished, we start to clean up quickly, my father barking orders as he hauls out the trash, the rest of us clearing up, doing dishes, wiping the table. Whatever else we may be, we are not a slovenly family. Soon Joe announces that he and Jay must get their things.

"You're not staying?" My eyebrows lift.

My uncle smiles slightly. "Dick, when you own a business, you don't take vacations. The lanes can't run themselves!" Together with Nellie Fox, Chicago's famous second baseman, he owns a prosperous bowling alley on the edge of Chambersburg, the Nellie Fox Bowl. My cousin, unsuited for most sorts of employment, works for his father at the lanes. "We have a tournament," Joe adds, wiping his glasses on his shirt. "It'll last through August."

My glance slides to my aunt. "Well, Vee—"

She looks at me levelly. "*I'm* staying," she says. She smiles, hugging Joe, patting him lightly on the fanny and kissing his cheek. "I'm going to let the men in the family go work."

My uncle invites me to come in to see the lanes. I promise that I will, at some point. Soon.

My aunt catches my eye as I'm making this promise. From a distance she regards her grown son and husband. Family rumor has it that my uncle has an assistant, a woman in her thirties, with whom he spends a lot of time out at the lanes.

My father announces that we'll walk them to the car. We round up the flashlights—by now night has fallen—and file out the door, our cones of light skittering across the grass in front of us. The usual copperhead precautions. Snakebite kits, complete with serum and syringes, are kept in the refrigerators of both the log house and the upper house.

It's a calm August night, the heat dropping now, although it's still warm enough. No breeze is stirring. The sky is thick with stars. I suck in a breath at the sight of it all, impressed by how brilliant our galaxy is out here in the mountains, with no light to dim it. On the other side of the lane the woods loom, dense and black.

Farewells are made. Joe's taillights wink and vanish as he heads out toward the road. Back indoors, we congregate in the kitchen.

Relieved of her family, Vee smiles as if refreshed and slides both palms down the sides of her shorts. She lights a cigarette and inhales quickly.

"Well!" says my mother. "That was just lovely!" Her tone seems to indicate that everything has concluded.

My eye catches my father's.

He pauses only slightly. "What a splendid night!" he says. "Let's go out and enjoy the porch. Find some candles. Let's have wine!"

We applaud the idea.

A jug of Chianti appears. Vee finds a pair of half-burned candles stuck in old bottles. We proceed to the porch, whose darkness enfolds us till someone lights a match. We seat ourselves again at the long picnic table, on whose surface the candlelight makes bright slanting puddles. The wine goes around.

The night breathes about us. Just enough air is coming in through the screens to nudge the flames sideways. The cicadas and tree frogs exchange their dry, raucous calls in the treetops, and the bullfrogs emit a steady thrum of croaks. So many night creatures emerge at this hour: the rabbits and the foxes, the mice and the blacksnakes. Raccoons. Opossums. A skunk might wander by, a deer drink from the pond.

The wine is going around when my father lifts his hand. "*Shh!* Stop! Listen!"

We halt, but hear nothing save the twang of the bullfrogs, the tree frogs and cicadas. Someone sets the wine softly down on the table.

"Ted, what is it?"

"Hush, Peg! Just listen!"

We fall silent. The candles flicker. Moths hurl themselves against the screens, wings thumping.

Suddenly it arrives from far off in the forest: the high, quick first syllable; the second, short, low one, almost like a grace note; the third, more sustained one that rises and falls, a breath exhaled, a mournful bugle. The sequence comes again.

"A whippoorwill," my father whispers.

We're about to start speaking, but he holds his hand up sharply. Our attention is stilled. The far call reaches us, faintly, for a third time. Then, like a miracle, from the branches of the ash tree just beyond the darkened screen: "*Whip-poor-WILL! Whip-poor-WILL!*" Our own bird, responding!

We sit in hushed silence, all seven of us, swapping pleasurable glances. Suddenly my father, his head at an angle, lifts his hand again. Once more it takes us a moment to hear it. A new voice has entered: it's the high, thrilling moan of—what? A distant horned owl. It's a sound more mournful, even, than the far-off whippoorwill.

While the three birds are calling, we look at my father. He sits with his head tilted. He's the author of all this: the birds, the splendid evening, this gathering on the porch. He has conjured this magic from his vast fund of power. This sacred place, this moment.

It's nonsense, of course, and we return to being people amid a buzz of conversation. The wine gets passed; the candles glitter. Then someone's voice declares, "It's a night for a swim!"

A moment's pause ensues before I acknowledge it as my own.

"*I'm* game!" Jen laughs.

Vee smiles. "Well, I must say, it's an interesting idea!"

"It's awfully dark," says Charlie.

"So? Who cares!" I tell him, feeling bold, independent. "The fish don't see any worse in the dark."

Steve says that he's willing.

Charlie says his suit is wet.

"Who needs suits?" I glance around the table at everyone but my father. Issuing a challenge.

"You know, I haven't gone skinny-dipping up here," Vee muses, her voice suddenly soft, "since Joe and I sneaked in one night after a picnic. That was, oh, ten years ago."

Charlie gives a short laugh, now that the idea is brewing. Steve, too, chuckles. Jen laughs a second time. It's down to Vee and me, then.

"I bet you're bashful," I say.

Vee looks at me from the other side of the table. She sends a plume of smoke at me, then lets her rounded lips widen into a smile. "I'm not someone that you want to dare, sonny."

"But I already have!" I smile back at her. Those rumors regarding Joe and his friend at the lanes—what the hell. Tit for tat.

My father has stayed silent throughout this exchange. He has sat so still I've been unaware of him until this moment.

My mother says now, in a bruised, edgy voice, "Why, I'd be afraid of snakes!"

This response somehow catalyzes my aunt. "Oh, Peggy!" Vee says. She exhales through her nose. "It's late enough now that all the snakes are probably gone." She lifts herself quickly to a standing position, her shoulders thrown back, her chest pushed forward. "So!" She grins. "Who's game?"

A whoop and a scuffle. The commotion makes the screened porch shake as we pile through the door. On the run, we grab towels from the clothesline out front.

I've had so much wine that the grass is a blur below the plane of my vision. I kick off my sneakers as soon as I hit the sand beach and start to shed my clothes. My aunt is right behind me. Despite the excitement of the moment, I turn away slightly as I'm dropping my trousers—from modesty or what, I can't say for sure; it just seems a reflex. This doesn't keep me, though, from getting a solid look at Vee, whose back still has the graceful taper of a girl's and whose snug butt I could cup in the palms of my hands. She has stripped before I have and pranced down to the water. She high-steps into the shallows and launches herself into a flat, graceful dive, a delicious flash of light that I witness from behind. I plunge in myself, unmindful of the others. My father, I realize, is nowhere in sight; I know in my bones that he has stayed at the house.

The cold water grips me. I respond with a quick gasp, a vulnerable shiver. Will I get nipped by bluegills? I buoy myself, treading in the warmer surface water, and glance around. Vee is five yards off, doing the crawl away from me; suddenly she stops, turns around, and treads water, her white teeth gleaming as she smiles in the starlight. Steve and Charlie have swum to the far side of the pond, more discernible as splashes than as a pair of dark heads. Jen is behind me, to my right. She swims toward me now, doing an easy breaststroke.

"Gee!" she says. "This is neat!"

As she nears me, streaks of bleary light glaze her eyes, and I realize that she's wearing her glasses in the water. "Jesus, Jen!" I exclaim. "For Christ's sake! When you're *swimming*—?"

"We-ell," she says with a grin, "I can't *see* without them." She gives a girlish laugh. "How do you float?"

"Back or front?"

"Either way."

I'm about to demonstrate when my mother's form catches my eye. I look up, surprised. She has taken up a post at the end of the dock, sitting on the narrow wooden bench along the handrail.

"Peggy," my aunt is saying, "why don't you join us? It's *wonderful* in the water."

"No sirree!" my mother answers. "I'm going to sit here and keep a good eye on things!"

So. The protectress has decided to take up the vigil. I might have guessed as much. Intuitively I know that the issue isn't Jen; it's my aunt. Old rivalries, perhaps, old wounds; at any rate, how would I know? Perfunctorily, on Jen's behalf, I demonstrate the technique for vertical floating—head tilted back, arms out, palms up, back arched very slightly—and then swim away from her, treading water in a warm spot off by myself.

Irritation overtakes me. Son of a bitch. I swim to the edge and climb out without looking back, grab my towel off the beach, and dress in seconds. The others follow. I'm the first indoors. Jen appears with my aunt, their faces pleased, their dark hair dripping. They've brought their towels into the house. My mother comes in last, face flushed, jaw tight.

"Folks, it's bedtime," says my father. "Charlie, you'll be staying at the upper house with Vee. I want you to be there in case she needs anything."

It's the first of several orders he gives concerning the sleeping arrangements. My mother will stay downstairs here with him, in the big double bed that unfolds in the living room, Jen, Steve, and I will be upstairs, in the back loft.

Before she leaves, Vee says, "Give your aunt a good-night kiss."

It's an awkward moment for me, since I know that her request is meant to spite my mother; it doesn't really have all that much to do with me. But I have no objection. I peck her cheek chastely; she gives me a smile. An electric thread seems to link the two of us.

Then she and Charlie leave amid a flurry of good-nights, flashlights in hand.

Jen, Steve, and I head off to the loft. My father calls to me as I'm starting up the stairs: "Dick, be sure that the back window is open and the screen well secured. Otherwise Jen will roast."

"Okay!" I shout.

The door to the living room is shut. Still, I think I hear my parents' voices, muffled as if by cotton:

"Ted, do you think Jen will have enough privacy up there?"

"For Christ's sake, woman! Don't fret about it. She has a whole loft to herself!"

"Well, I just want to be sure she'll be comfortable, that's all . . ."

But maybe this isn't anything I really hear. Maybe I only imagine it.

There's a dormitory rustle and a shy laugh from Jen as the three of us settle in. Steve and I are sleeping in the front half of the loft, on twin steel cots that stand some six feet apart; Jen is in the back half, on one of two cots in the narrower section there. A doorway with no door separates the halves. For all intents and purposes, the loft is one room.

It's hot up here. The strong smell of mothballs from the old blanket chests gives the loft a familiar odor that carries me back across the years. Once the lights are out, I peel off my T-shirt, leaving my shorts on, and lie on the top sheet, my skin in a light sweat. Things seem unreal. Here I am now, exactly where I vowed I *wouldn't* be—wouldn't let myself be. I've let myself become distracted, unmindful of my need to seek—well, what?

These thoughts are interrupted by a shuffle downstairs. I recognize the footfalls and the nature of the movements: it's my father, in the kitchen. He's putting something away, or remembering to set something out for tomorrow morning. Soon his sounds die away. He has gone back to bed, shutting the door to the living room.

My eyes roam, but I see nothing. Darkness is impenetrable up here on moonless nights; once all the lights are off, you can't see a hand in front of your face. It has always bothered me, this absolute darkness. My father forbids night-lights: *"You sleep better,"* he says, *"if you sleep in the dark."* No one dares cross him.

It's frugality, partly. For me, the worst of it is the old fear that afflicts me. In August a certain type of thick, mottled spider takes to spreading its web across windows and porch corners. Grass spiders, too—some large enough, it seems, to be wolf spiders—will migrate indoors, looking for insects; and of course there are the cousins of the deadly black widow, which prefer bathroom crannies, obscure windowsills, and screened porch enclosures as spots to build their webs. I loathe it when a spider runs over me at night or when I wake in the morning with a badly puffed lip.

My ears compensate for the lack of visibility. The night here is layered. There's the intermittent swish of a lone car passing on Route 75, several hundred yards off; the ruckus of the bullfrogs; the steadier din of the tree frogs and cicadas; and then, closer in, the soft bump of large moths landing against the screens in their blind pursuit of nothing, the chirp of the crickets that have found their way indoors.

The innermost layer contains the sounds that we make—Jen, Steve, and I. My own breathing is audible in this warm night air; I am careful not to sigh, or to exhale too loudly. Bedsprings creak whenever someone moves or turns, and a yawn or sneeze will betray someone's presence. Mainly I hear silence.

A cough, a deliberate cough, disrupts the darkness, and I am lifted from my pallet by invisible hands. The window by Jen's cot! I must make sure it's open. My feet find the broad ancient floorboards at my bedside and I float, like a ghost, through the doorway to the back of the loft.

"Jen," I say matter-of-factly. "I've got to open the window to make sure you have air."

I speak at normal volume to foster the pretense that there's no stealth involved. I feel my way to the window. The cooler outdoor air sifts against my bare chest. The window is already open. A piece from a broom handle is wedged against the sash to hold it in place.

Jen makes her move. She has risen from her mattress and come up behind me; when I turn, she's there waiting—not so much waiting as in full, deliberate motion. Her arms encircle me at mid–chest level, and the next thing I know, her mouth has found mine, her tongue plunging in. More than anything else, what I experience is her bulk, the anomaly of being a slender man bumping up against so large a woman. At a loss, I grapple with her, my mouth against hers, my arms around her shoulders. I'm impressed by how muscular her body is. How solid.

I feel oddly light, as though my feet are off the ground. Still, something about this matter requires my compliance. Jen and I jerk and shuffle our way toward the bed, two novice dancers. She drags me—I drag her—while we fumble with each other. She tugs at my shorts while my hands grope her clothing. She's wearing a sweatshirt, a bra, and tights. The impulse seizes me to undo her bra from inside her sweatshirt. The hook comes undone, but I get the straps tangled; the next thing I know, I'm lost in a maze. Jen lets go of me and takes a step back. I can sense her undoing the damage in the dark. When we close again, she's naked, her skin warm and damp. Her mouth finds mine. She takes my hand in hers and guides it in. She's so wet between her legs that there seems no distinction between outside and inside; my fingers slither in and, after a second's random pushing, meet a hardish rim of rubber. Her diaphragm. Jesus. Her tongue seems to consume me. I back off to catch my breath. "What do you want?" Jen whispers.

"I don't know!" I answer. My voice comes out as a small, hoarse croak. Jen's hand finds my cock. Then we've landed on the mattress and she's reaching down and pulling me impatiently inside her. I'm half hard at best, though as I begin moving in her, I feel myself strengthen. Jen reaches back and plants her hands on my butt, bucking to get a better purchase. *She's impatient!* I think. *I'm not doing it right.* And with that I subside. Deflate. Go limp on her.

"What do you want?" she says again, into my ear. I wince. Her breath tickles, and I roll off her belly, amazed by how massive she is underneath me. I stare into the darkness. The next thing I know, she has leaned over and put my limp cock into her mouth, her tongue busy on it. I cannot respond. I lie there in silence, submitting to her effort for perhaps thirty seconds, willing myself, *willing*, to respond, to grow aroused. I feel some wish, even, to give Jen pleasure—anything, something!—but the impulse merely seems to float away from me. My body is an abstraction, a hollowed-out husk, all the juices removed. I cannot feel a thing.

I'm about to squirm away when Jen desists. She knows it's not working. Her head rests on my stomach. I put my hand on her shoulder and encourage her to move up. For a second I lie there in the dark, my arm across her waist.

"Jen, I'm sorry," I murmur. "I'm just not up for this."

A long pause follows. "Okay," she whispers.

"But maybe—" I begin.

"Okay," she says finally.

I retreat to my bed, my weight dropping heavily onto it, and stare at the ceiling. Numbness descends. A few seconds pass before bedsprings near me squeal. Feet shuffle. A brief silence. The next thing I hear is a soft, rhythmic rocking in the other part of the loft, a creaking of springs that swells toward a protest. Suddenly Jen lets out a hard, sudden gasp and the creaking noise ceases. "Oh, my!" she exclaims. A pause, then the verdict. "I never knew before, Steve, that you were such a *man!*"

My brother gives a chuckle, the kind of sound he makes when he's told a joke he relishes. I don't have a sense that he's competing with me, although he could well be. He's just pleased with himself.

He and Jen talk in tones so low that I can't hear what they say. I'm just as happy not to. Numbness has spread all the way to my toes now. I peer into the darkness. What strikes me especially about Jen's exclamation is—well, of course I can't help dwelling on the "such a *man!*" part, which is pointed enough. But it's the first part of her comment that snags my attention. "*I never knew before . . .*"

Is there some *history* here, some prior involvement? Have I stepped into the middle of much more than I've realized during this weekend? What the hell's going *on?* How much of this is *staged?* Has my father been—

Suddenly Steve returns. He settles into his bed without making a sound. I find this tactful. No prolonged, loud sighs or shows of evident satisfaction. He just stays quiet.

I pick up the thread. Yes. Jesus. My father . . . our talk this afternoon. His suggesting that we have wine, so uncharacteristic of him; his staying clear of the pond while we were out there this evening; his telling me to be sure that Jen's window is open. It was *already* open, that stout piece of broomstick wedged against the sash by someone's strong hand . . .

How does this all add up?

I roll onto my side, my head spinning slightly. So, then . . . My mind stops. "Staged." The word returns to me. I'd allowed myself to fancy, though I'd truly known better, that Jen's availability was . . . I can't even think it. Of course. How stupid. Scarcely spontaneous!

My father's strong hand.

And yet, and yet, if this is so, what does it imply about his relationship with Jen, and her relationship with him, that she would do this, and do this so willingly, for him?

A deep, forbidden precinct is opened to view, one I cannot bear to make my way into. Beyond the fierce control being exercised here, there lies . . . what?

I stop.

I'm brought back into the room by a thudding sensation. At first I mistake it for Steve's rising again for another go at Jen. It takes me a second to identify its source, which consists of my own heart. My heart's in an uproar, a fist shooting marbles or thrashing at something. I groan. Inhale sharply. Roll over on my back to ease the pressure on my ribs. I'm going to fly out of myself.

And my mother—what does *she* know? Is Jen doing this with *her* implicit sanction? Was I right when I'd thought, earlier, about my parents as being people who . . . ?

I come back to the present. The darkness swirls around me. It occurs to me, rather bitterly, that whatever Steve is feeling now, he's perfectly welcome to it.

I should have fled.

It's a bright day outside. As I take my first bearings, I squint at the gleaming whitewash that covers the walls. Both my sheet and my blanket have slid to the floor. I've slept on my stomach, one knee hiked up toward my belly, the way young children sleep. Turning my gaze over my shoulder, I peer down my length. What I mainly see is my bare heel and my ankle. Such primitive constructions. Dinosaur bones found in some swampy tar pit.

I struggle out of bed. The commotion of breakfast fills the kitchen below me. Strong scents of bacon and freshly brewed coffee come up through the floorboards. Except for me, the loft is empty. How late have I slept?

I feel hunger, hunger and dread at having to join the others. I'm not at all sorry I couldn't get it on with Jen; that my body subverted me is evidence, I take it, of my inward resistance. But I've failed both ways: at being good *and* being bad. The worst shilly-shallying.

As I clomp downstairs, I'm suddenly reminded of several things about myself: that I'm a father; that I'm still a husband, even in the midst of a divorce; that I'm a graduate student, a scholar. God. How many of my roles I've compromised in the course of one day!

My mother is first to greet me. "Why, Buck!" she says. "Good morning." She comes over and kisses me. "Did you sleep well last night?"

"Yeah. Fine," I mutter.

She stands there smiling, her face extra-cheery. That she has used this old nickname and asked such a question—how inscrutable I find her!

Someone else greets me in a low, amused voice. I look up. It's Vee. She's seated at the big indoor table, smoking and holding a hot mug of coffee. I see in an instant that her amusement is merely friendly. I feel grateful to her.

When I glance at my father, he looks away from me. His eyes meet Steve's briefly. They are seated next to each other at the opposite end of the table from Vee. Charlie sits off by himself, sullen and red-eyed. Jen is on the screened porch rinsing out something at the sink. When she steps into the kitchen, her eyes drop. Conspirators, all four of us. Even if, at this point, I'm the odd man out.

The next few minutes are scarcely pleasant. My mother asks if I want any breakfast, offering to warm up some eggs and bacon for me. Vee hands me coffee, which I willingly accept. My mind quickly slides back to last night's swim.

Finally there's my father. He is wearing, again, his usual summer outfit—the filthy old ball cap, the frayed tennis shoes, the drooping bathing trunks, the scruffy white T-shirt. His manner is furtive, hooded. He suggests that we try to get in some fishing this morning, or maybe drive up to Cowans Gap for a hike (an idea I nix: my drive back's a long one). Then he asks if I'd be willing to lend him a hand with some chores. I nod yes while thinking, *How the hell could he have known that I'd never be a hitter, all those many years ago?*

And, as suddenly as I've come, I'm gone.

The valley unfolds its late-summer magic as I drive east on Route 75 toward the turnpike. Cornfields. Meadows. Pastures thick with cattle. Blue sky, towering clouds. The high flanking mountains, intensely green in their forests. God's country, no question. A chunk of the world I know like the back of my hand.

Then why, *why, WHY?*

I swerve off the road on the crest of a hill as I swing into Fannettsburg—a scattering of houses, a roadside restaurant, and a bleak gas station. My tires crunch on gravel. I stagger out, breathe, and exhale steeply. My eye travels out into the deep summer sunshine. The clouds to the east have the flat, beveled bottoms and plumed, puffy crests that promise no rain.

It seems so very clear, now, what has happened this weekend. There has been no ambush; I have not been victimized without my consent. The cost is what stuns me. I have sold myself short. Lost a friendship I have valued. Demeaned myself before my brother. Destroyed, in the process, a long-cherished fiction of being different, somehow—different from my family. Of knowing better, of wanting better. I've squandered any respect I might have had for myself, held back in reserve from all my other great follies. My fingertips tingle. I can feel the blood drain from my lips.

I climb into the car and swing out toward the turnpike.

TRANSITIONS

"Well, not yet," my father is saying. "But I'm starting to think about it." He lifts his chin slightly. "This next post of mine is probably going to be my last."

"You'd *retire*?" I say, incredulous.

"Dick!" he says firmly. "It's one of the fine arts in life to know when to quit. I'll be fifty next August."

"Yeah, but—"

"Hear me out! Please." He shifts in his chair. "The foreign service is 'downsizing'—that frightful new word! It started while Kennedy was still in office; for all his initiative in founding the Peace Corps, he was of the new breed in his foreign policy stance. The old-style diplomacy we practiced is dying. The Peace Corps is really a publicity stunt—although a good one, I'll grant you."

He pauses, then continues. "Other things call to me. My scholarship, mainly. You know that I've affiliated myself with the Smithsonian—"

"No," I say. "I didn't know that."

"Oh, I have! In the capacity of a 'research associate.' It's their catchall term for an unsalaried scholar working under their imprimatur. When I retire, I'll have an office. Access to resources. An institutional base. Why, they're already funding most of my trips to the Middle East! I've begun a quest, you know, for the source of Bronze Age tin. It promises to be a fairly massive undertaking. We *know* where the copper in the ancient world comes from, but tin, you see—"

He stops himself.

Taking advantage of his pause, I say that I'd have thought (this is why the idea of early retirement surprised me) that he would want, now, to enjoy the benefits of his seniority. "Given your rank, after all—"

"Oh, hell, I'm a congressional appointee. That's not the point."

"The point, then, is—?"

"To be honest, Dick, it's just time for me to get out." My father looks at me. His mouth goes sour, a gesture halfway between disgust and resignation. "I haven't been the easiest of people in the government. I've gone my own way, largely. You'll recall how I resisted being sent overseas . . . I wanted all you boys to have your childhood in the States, though it didn't quite work out that way for Steve and Charlie. Then, you know, out in Iran, I ran afoul of Bob Lincoln. He was regional foreign service chief at the time."

"No, I didn't. What happened?"

"He convened a meeting of us—all of the region's cultural affairs officers—in Beirut every year. He asked for suggestions; wanted to know if there was anything we ought to be doing. So I made a suggestion—a very constructive one, I thought. But he took it very personally. He was a queer sort of fellow. 'Make that *your* project, Ted!' he said. Well, hell, I couldn't have; what I'd suggested would have been too big for my office alone to manage. After that, he denied me my in-grade raises the whole time I was out there. David was sympathetic; David Nalle, you'll recall, was director of the Iran-America Society at the time. *He* thought I was one of the two best CAOs we had in the field.

"But there are other, deeper reasons. We lack a global will now. Our leaders have lost their vision. They don't understand how crucial the U.S. is! World peace and stability *cannot exist* without us. It's not a role we've looked for; it's been thrust upon us historically. You see, this 'downsizing' I mentioned is a symptom of the new trends. I have colleagues now—fiercely dedicated people, old foreign service hands—returning from overseas to discover that they have literally no place to go! Oh, they're still drawing salaries; they still have their 'rank'; but they're dispossessed persons! They aren't given offices; they have no new assignments. They don't even have a place to hang their hats! They're wandering the halls of the Agency like ghosts. Some of the poor devils haven't grasped yet what's hit them.

"*I'd* seen this coming! And I wasn't at all ready to be a casualty of it. The best of patriots—you know I've always said this—plants one foot outside the group that he's loyal to. So I'll take this new appointment as cultural officer in Athens, though it grieves me to uproot your mother and Charlie again. Charlie especially. It doesn't please me, either, that this junta is in power. But then, that may be it!"

We're finished with this subject. It's plain enough to me that my father has pronounced his final word on the matter.

I'm trying to figure out how I feel about all this—I'm visiting my parents in their home in North Arlington; it's a cold December day, just days before Christmas 1968, at the end of my very first semester of teaching—when my father says suddenly, "And *you've* begun to make your way in academia now!"

I laugh at this, uncomfortably. There's something about his tone that I don't quite get. "Yes. Well. '*Begun.*' Exactly!"

"You'll get your degree in—?"

"June. Around my birthday. That is, *if* I get my dissertation in on time. It's due May 1."

"I'm sure you will," he says.

I acknowledge that I'm plugging away at it pretty hard. But I tread lightly here. My father had been a doctoral candidate at Johns Hopkins in the early 1940s; then John, Steve, and I were born in quick succession, the country entered the war, and he never quite managed to complete his degree. Mine will be the first Ph.D. in the family.

"Of course," says my father, his voice quite casual, "once you're all finished, you might want to look around. Survey the broader canvas."

"Survey?"

"Other fields!"

I'm perplexed. "Well, after all, my degree *is* in English. I don't know what else . . ."

"That's the thing," says my father, "about the academic world. It makes you a narrow specialist! Which is *fine*, of course. Initially. At some later point, though, you'll want to broaden out."

"My interests *are* diverse," I say, confused, on the defensive. "It's not as though I'm interested in just one thing."

My father is willing to drop the subject now. "Sure," he says. "I'm sure you're not! . . . And then, you and Marcia are planning your wedding for when?"

"June. Two years still. Right after *she* graduates. I hope all of you will be able to come!"

"We won't miss it. I assure you."

I switch subjects now. "By the way, Mom had said something about a new mountain property you're thinking of buying. Tell me about it."

"Why, yes!" my father says, and rotates his shoulders. "There are several I might bid on. One's up toward Bedford; another's out the road up beyond Cowans Gap, not far from Burnt Cabins . . ."

"Pennsylvania, then."

"Oh, surely!"

A question suddenly hits me I hadn't thought of before. I smile as I ask it. "So, what about the mountain place?"

"Well, it's gotten so crowded up there, you know. So hectic . . ." My father must be reading the expression on my face, because his jaw juts forward and his eyes flare at me. His tone goes stiff. "One feels that one is ready for a place of one's own!"

"Huh!" I say, and go dumb. The idea that he would like, now, to set himself apart, find a place that isolates him from the rest of the family—I'm suddenly made to feel that my childhood has ended, that a loss has been incurred. The irony of it is not wasted on me. That *I* would feel this way—*I*, who for so many years had felt put upon because of all the hard work the mountain place had cost us . . .

I'm forced to confront the hard, simple fact: I'd grown to like the place.

More than just like it.

And he no longer does, not as he used to—though *he* had been the one who had urged the family to buy it in the early 1950s.

My father has swung back to his earlier subject. He would like, he says, to build himself a new house for retirement; not an ordinary house, but something special, unusual. They've already put some money away, he tells me, just a little each month. He has a few ideas forming: it would be quite grand, provide a new family base . . .

"Maybe," he concludes, his smile focused on me, "you could come out and join me for a glance at some of the places that I have my eye on! If you have an inclination. Before we set sail for Greece."

I have an odd, smudged feeling as I make my departure. It's a familiar sensation of having props kicked out from under me, but without my fully knowing what the props have been, exactly.

This feeling slips in beneath my light windbreaker and mixes with the cold as I get into my car. The weather threatens snow. The car is brand-new, a Volvo, one of several transitions: my appointment as a professor, my engagement to Marcia, my being near the completion of my Ph.D. . . . I've moved now to New Jersey; my children are growing up here in Arlington, where my ex-wife lives; they're getting big quickly—Michele's already seven, my son, Kent, almost six, although I'm three years shy of thirty. My debts are lessening, finally, now that I'm drawing a salary.

But the transitions aren't all—as I've seen today!—on my side. Once I've said my good-byes and set myself on the road north, I can't help thinking, *Dick, what were you expecting—that the world would stand still? That only YOU would change?* I should have known better. About a great many things.

FATES IN THE MAKING

"I can't help wondering if God hasn't put some kind of curse on this family."

The words of Grandma Wertime from back in the old days, when the patterns of emotional disorder in the family had become too clear to ignore any longer. So many of her grandchildren with emotional problems! The *sons* in the clan in particular. One child at least, it seemed, in virtually every family, except perhaps for the Wehausens, Kay and John's family . . .

That I feel guilty toward Charlie—is that any wonder? One day at the mountain place, when Charlie is two and still sleeps in a crib (I'm twelve at the time), he awakes from his nap sometime in midafternoon. "Dick," my mother says, "please go in and change Charlie."

"Why the hell should I?" I say.

"Please," she says, "don't argue."

"Shit," I grumble, scowling.

"Please don't use that word," she says.

As I get up and trudge inside—the family's been outdoors, sitting in the yard; we're staying at the upper house—I can feel it already: that ominous tingle, as if mice are running up and down my forearms. Since the time he turned one, Charlie has been sleeping in Steve's and my bedroom, where *I'm* the one expected to tend to his needs in the dead of night. *Why not John, goddammit? HE'S the older brother!* Steve's too young; I understand that. So it's always left to me to see that Charlie's changed and dry, and has had his nightly bottle. Clearly my mother doesn't want to deal with him. When he begins crying at night, she's so far away downstairs, in that big bedroom of theirs, in another part of the apartment . . .

Charlie's a screamer. He cries so hard that the veins in his neck and temples stand out. He becomes disfigured.

My rage suddenly darkens. I lean forward over the crib and slap his face. He screams. I hit him even harder. The next thing I

know, I've shoved a pillow against his face and am standing there pressing my full weight against it. I find myself transfixed by the daring of my action, by the pure, clean evil of it, and watch unmoved while my brother kicks and writhes.

I count off the seconds. How long does it take, exactly, to suffocate someone? Then the moment is over. A cold fear grips me; I fling aside the pillow. I gather Charlie up, cradling him in my arms while he gasps and cries and shivers. I rock him, I murmur. When he has calmed—it takes time—I change his diaper carefully and carry him outside. My whole body's shaking. *Jesus Christ, Dick! What in the hell were you doing?*

I can't help noting that no one has intervened. For all the noise we've made.

This memory recurs, almost twenty years later, during the weeks that Marcia and I are doing our best to help Charlie. It's 1972.

Early February. We live in New Brunswick, where I'm teaching at Rutgers. Charlie is here now.

How he's come to stay with us is a somewhat tangled story. Late last summer he'd returned to Athens after a long trip to India that my parents had permitted. He'd been accompanied by a friend of his, a boy named Nick. They traveled for five months.

To my mind, my parents (I couldn't speak for Nick's parents) were remiss in letting Charlie undertake such a journey. Two teenage boys wandering unsupervised through Turkey, Iran, Afghanistan, and Pakistan on their way to *India*, of all places!—a recipe for disaster. Luckily for everyone, they'd both returned safely. But the conflicts my parents had been experiencing with Charlie, the ones that had made them so indulgent to begin with in letting him head off to the Indian subcontinent, had reemerged quickly. What surprise in that? They weren't addressing any of Charlie's real problems, to which his troubled conduct (his lack of discipline, his surly unruliness, his indifference to his schoolwork) stood obviously much more as symptoms than as causes.

So when my mother and my father phoned us from Athens and asked us if Charlie could "come visit for a spell"—a month or two, maybe—right away we said yes.

We could *help* Charlie, somehow, Marcia and I! We had enjoyed his company during our first trip to Greece in the summer of '69—the three of us knocked around the Plaka, and had toured the Acropolis on a brutally hot day—and felt that we had achieved a good rapport with him. Marcia was very fond of Charlie, fonder than she was of my other brothers, and saw him somewhat as the little brother she'd never had.

Charlie's stay with us has begun well enough. We've shown him around; reminisced over supper about our trips out to Greece in '69 and '71; heard in more detail about his odyssey to India, where he'd lived in an ashram on a diet of rice and vegetables, studied meditation, and pored over works like the Tibetan Book of the Dead. He tells us funny stories about the visits he and Nick had paid to the marijuana fields in the Afghan countryside, where the pot plants grow as high as small olive trees.

But our apartment's cramped; Charlie is sleeping on the sofa in our living room, his clothes strewn about. After a week it becomes apparent that he can't stay with us the entire time if he'll be here for a couple of months. We look for a rental room. He's quite understanding; he, too, needs some privacy, and is hopeful that he'll start meeting people around the campus. There's no lack of people his age in New Brunswick.

We secure him a room in the home of an older woman, just six blocks from us. Sparsely furnished, his upstairs room has a hot plate, fridge, and sink. Charlie could start, we say, to do some cooking for himself. He gets settled in, though he still comes to our place for supper most nights. I often see him around town, out on one of his walks—he's a constant, tireless walker—and feel that the tide might start to turn for him.

I'm wrong about this. Snow and ice arrive; with the onset of the weather, Charlie starts to take a plunge. First he begins dropping in on us at all hours, his face red with windburn, his hands and fingers numb from the bitter, blustery cold. We get him some gloves. He asks if he can't spend the night on our sofa; his room is poorly heated, he's very lonely there, and bad dreams afflict him. I can see that he's sleepless: his eyes have grown bloodshot; he's become restless, nervous. At first we resist his request, not wishing to set a pattern. I spend more time with him over in his room, which is littered with copies of *Playboy* and *Penthouse*. Food lies around, half eaten and undisposed of.

I'm reminded by the food of an incident that had occurred some months earlier: Charlie had made a quick trip to the States at summer's end, right after his sojourn in India. He'd stopped in September to spend two days with us, but Marcia was away seeing her parents at the time, so I hosted him alone. His hair had grown long, and he wore a goatee; he had also lost so much weight in India that he looked rather Christlike. His eyes shone, and his speech had a feverish brilliance to it. He urged me to undertake the study of Hinduism and talked a great deal about karma and mantras. I came home one afternoon—I'd been off teaching—to discover him standing right inside my front door. He had warmed some baked beans in a saucepan and was standing there scarfing them down as I entered. No problem in itself; he needed to be eating. But while he stood there, spooning beans into his mouth, he stared at me vacantly, as if I weren't there. He was oblivious as well to the sticky brown trail that ran back across the floor all the way into the kitchen. The incident had disturbed me, but at that time I'd just written it off as carelessness.

I know that life in Athens has not been easy for Charlie. It's his second time in exile; the first, in Tehran, began when he was eight. In both cities he's had to live in a fortified dwelling—first the high-walled compound, heavily gated, in Iran; now, in Athens, a villa in the suburbs, where lemon trees canopy the well-tended lawns but a steel fence surrounds the whole place for security; a house nearby, also rented by a diplomat, has recently been the target of terrorist bombs. He feels that his years as a teen are being wasted. At least in Athens he has freedom—and friends. Peter Blood. Nick. Arthur. Stephanie. Others. All transients, however: children of diplomats or international businessmen, they're likely, as he is, to move away in a minute.

And my parents aren't easy. My mother's preoccupied with her social life in Athens, my father with his duties there as cultural attaché. There's also his womanizing, which just this past year has found him involved in a damaging affair with the wife of a very wealthy Greek-American tycoon. I don't know how much Charlie knows about this affair (my father filled my ears with it during *our* last visit, fatuously claiming that his sexual drives and needs put him in what he called "the ninety-ninth percentile"), but my parents' indifference to his problems and his welfare have clearly had a very bad effect on my brother.

I remind myself of all this, and of my early guilt toward Charlie, as the winter wears on. But things get no better. He reports terrible nightmares—dreams in which rats are gnawing on his fingers; he can't shake them off, however frantically he tries—and his weight is ballooning; he is stuffing himself, it seems, with doughnuts and pastries to salve his loneliness. He's made social overtures to a number of young people, but they've all rebuffed him. It isn't hard to see why: his eyes have a desperate, hungry, overly eager look. When I see him out on one of his many walks, he looks driven. Haunted.

"Dick," Marcia says one day in early March, "we've got to do something."

I take a deep breath. I've seen this coming.

"We've done very our best, but it's not working out."

"Yeah. We're trying, Lord knows."

My being agreeable doesn't satisfy my wife. "It's wrecking both of us! We've only been married for *eight months*, for God's sake! Since he started coming over here to sleep on the couch again—you should never have given in on that!—he's been playing those awful records till *three in the morning* . . . or else he gets in the tub in the middle of the night for one of his baths and leaves the place a total mess!"

In the mornings we discover both the bathmat and the towels lying soaked on the floor, the tub still full of water, a fresh cake of soap dissolving in the middle. Clothes strewn about, as soaked as the towels. And the records he plays—by the Grateful Dead, Led Zeppelin, and the like. Their weird, spooky melodies and equally troubling lyrics come sifting through the walls to disrupt our sleep. One song, especially, sends chills up my spine: supposedly a hymn about Zen meditation, it repeats, over and over, "*Ahh-OOMM! Ahh-OOMM!*"—to the point where my head swims and my stomach turns over.

"I'll talk to Charlie," I tell her.

Which I do. It goes badly. It embarrasses him to learn that he's creating such a mess, and he promises to amend, but he's incapable of it. The bathroom chaos continues. His clothes lie everywhere. I have to do extra washes. I put restrictions on him about playing his albums in the middle of the night, but we continue to awake to the sounds of "*Ahh-OOMM!*"

At last I say, "Charlie, this just isn't working. You'll have to start sleeping at your own place again."

It's mid-March by now. Bitter weather has continued, a cloudy gloom maintaining its tough grip on New Brunswick. Not only have we endured the messes and records, we have listened to Charlie talk at increasing length about his dreams and his fantasies and the Tibetan Book of the Dead, which he can't seem to put out of his mind for more than a minute.

We're in over our heads, and finally ready to admit it. Perhaps Charlie senses this, knows in his bones that we've reached a terminus with him. He and I are in the doorway between the kitchen and our bedroom when I make the declaration that he'll have to start sleeping at his own place. His face grows red; he gives me a half smile. Then he throws a fake punch at me. I flinch, involuntarily. He grins, satisfied.

I'm on the phone with my father in less than ten minutes. Static interrupts us, but it doesn't deter me. "*Get back here right away! This is yours to handle now. You'll have to come over.*"

My father arrives within twenty-four hours. My mother reaches Kennedy two days later. I say to my parents, "I'm sorry about all this, but we did our best."

"You couldn't have known!" says my mother. "Why, you and Marcia have only been married—what?"

"Eight months."

As I turn away from my parents, I am filled with a grim sense of futility, depression. And my old guilt toward Charlie . . .

THREE

A PHONE CALL

Early March, 1977. My mother's voice sounds higher than usual. I haven't talked to her in weeks at this point, so all the old strangeness of my conversations with her is suddenly fresh to me.

"Dick," she says, "do you have a minute?"

"Sure!" I say. "What's up?"

As soon as I've spoken, I regret my robustness. Something is afoot, and my mother is unhappy.

"Oh, I just need to talk. I've had a disappointment."

"I'm sorry to hear it."

"It's your father," she says.

A pause follows.

I wait.

"Well, you remember—" she begins. She stops herself. "I'm sorry. I'm just so upset."

I say, "Take your time. There's no hurry. Please."

"Thank you. Well . . . You know, Dick, I scarcely even know where to begin!"

"Wherever you want to."

She jumps into the middle by telling me how my father had begun sounding funny when she was on the phone with him. This was nearly a month ago. He's been working on his new house up above McConnellsburg, living for convenience at the mountain place. It's two valleys over. She's down in Fairlington, taking care of Grandma Schultz and also looking after Charlie, who's at loose ends.

". . . So I say to him, 'Ted, shall I drive up this weekend? We can get some time together.' After all, Dick, we hadn't seen each other for—oh, golly, what?—*five weeks*. Not since the New Year. Thinking, of course, you know, that it was the right thing to *do*. I'm not particularly crazy about the mountain place—you know that. No . . . So. Anyhow. He says to me—and his voice was rather odd—'How about some other weekend? I'm very busy right now.'

"'I'm very busy.' Can you *imagine*? Of course, you know, at first I thought he was busy with the house—no, that's not true, really; I really shouldn't say that." She laughs bleakly. "I guess I'm just trying to save myself some of the pain. Because right *away* I knew that there was something fishy about it.

"So I said to him, 'Well, all right, Ted . . . But what are you busy *with*?' He hesitated briefly. And you know, Dick, I could *swear*—could have sworn at the time—that there was someone there with him. I could just *feel* it, somehow. I almost thought I heard somebody in the background. Though I might have made that up.

"So I repeated my question. 'Ted, what are you busy *with*?' And he gave me a vague answer about his working very hard. So I said, 'Well, you know, I could always come up and help you!' After all, I'm not a weakling. And he answered no, it was better if I stayed down here.

"So I asked him, 'Ted, do you have someone there *with* you?' He got quite gruff with me! 'No!' he said. 'Of course not! Who would I have here?' 'Well,' I said, 'your brothers and sisters. Some of the family could be there!' And he said no, there wasn't . . . though he added that Aunt Clara had stopped by for a day, with David and Jackie.

"Well, that's how *that* phone conversation ended. I was frankly confounded. And at first, you know, Dick, I made all these efforts to ignore my intuitions; I said to myself how hard your father was probably working, how preoccupied he was . . . But still, I just had this *sense!* At first I felt confused; then I felt very hurt. And then (you know, I'm really kind of slow and stupid in these matters) I got quite angry! I decided then and there that I wouldn't sit back on my heels. No sirree! I was just too suspicious—yes, you're right!" My mother laughs. "I *did* have grounds, given his history, didn't I? Well, isn't that the limit!

"So you know what I did? I went on ahead and drove the devil up to McConnellsburg that very weekend! Without so much as even calling. Oh, it was quite a scene that followed! Just as soon as I came up over the hill at the top there—you know how steep it is; no, the driveway's no better, it's exactly the same now. . . . Anyhow, your father, just as soon as he saw me, came *running* out to the car and hopped into it. Hopped in! Right next to me! 'You know,' he said, without so much as greeting me, 'we're not getting any younger at this point. I think that we ought to have an open marriage.'"

"He actually *said* that to you?"

"Yes! In those exact words! 'I think we ought to have an open marriage.' Well, of course, as you can imagine, I didn't know what he *meant!* So I asked him. I said, 'Ted, what do you mean, *open marriage?*' He was at a loss, frankly, as to what to say next.

"But not for long! He was wearing this strange, peculiar look on his face. It was a very cold day. 'Why,' he said, 'I think that we ought to be able to see other people.' Well, at *that*, I said, 'Ted, we'll discuss this *indoors!*' I got out on my side.

"Well, boy, *that* made him nervous! He jumped out on *his* side and came around to me. He actually put himself between me and the house! 'I have a colleague here,' he said. 'A *good* colleague. A friend.' 'Well, then,' I said, 'sweetheart, *introduce* him to me!'"

I laugh, interrupting. "My God, what a scene!"

My mother laughs too, in a complicit-sounding way.

"Don't get me wrong," I tell her. "I'm not making light of it."

"Oh, you haven't heard the worst of it!" she says, her voice eager. "Wait'll you hear the *rest* of it!"

"That's quite a line, though — 'Well, then, *introduce* him to me!'"

"Isn't that *stupid* of me, Dick? I'm so naive sometimes! Well, anyway," says my mother, having paused to laugh again. "Though it isn't very funny. At the time, I must say, it was really *quite* painful."

"I can imagine," I say.

"Yes. So anyhow, your father says to me, 'Well, my colleague's not a *man*.' 'Well, then,' I ask, 'who *is* it?'

"Before he's even said a word, this strange woman appears around the edge of the house! Dick, I practically dropped my *jaw!* Here's this rail-thin woman — *skinny!* — with dyed black hair and a frightful-looking face, her eyes black with mascara — and all she's wearing, despite the bitter-cold weather, is a pair of black panty hose and a kind of brassiere top — a 'halter,' I guess you call them. Not another stitch on! And the panty hose. My word! You could see right *through* them!

"So while I'm standing there, gazing at this frightful-looking creature (Dick, she's really quite something! I think she must be ill, in fact, perhaps anorexic), she walks right up and puts her hand out to me. 'Hello! I'm Joan,' she says.

"'Well!' I said on the spot. '*I'm* Peggy Wertime. What are *you* doing here?'"

I can't help laughing into the phone when I hear this. "Good for you!" I say.

"Of course, your *father* has to get back into the conversation; maybe he thought I'd take a swing at Joan or something—"

"You should have!" I say, laughing.

"Well, of course you know I wouldn't have done a thing like that . . . But he jumps in again and says, 'Joan's been coming up to help me build the house.' 'Oh, is that right?' I say. 'And for how long has this been?'

"I must pause to tell you, Dick, that this woman has a deep voice, just like a man's! A *very* deep voice. So when she said 'I'm Joan' like that, at first I didn't know what to make of her!

"But your father doesn't answer me, at least not directly. 'Joan works with me at the Smithsonian,' he tells me. 'She's an expert in cement.' Well, of course I didn't really understand that for a minute; later on, I'd discover that she really *is* an expert—she's a very bright woman, I *will* give her credit for that . . . No, an expert in cement. Yes. Ancient cement, especially, the kind the Greeks and Romans used . . . She's a help to your father with his scholarly work, no question.

"But *anyway*, I finally had the presence of mind to say—not to her, but your father (jeepers, I didn't even want to *look* at her!)—'But this colleague of yours doesn't have proper clothes on!'"

Laughter pours from me into the phone.

My mother joins in. "Your father—it was really quite a scene, I have to tell you!—*scowled* at me for having dared to say this in front of Joan. And boy, did he ever dress me down for saying that later!

"'We've been sunning,' Joan tells me. Yes! Like that: 'We've been sunning.'

"'Look, Peg,' says your father. He actually took me by the elbow and led me back to the car! 'This is something you and I will have to discuss at some point later.' And frankly, Dick, that broke me. I just didn't have the will then to fight it any further."

"So, what did you do?"

"Then?" says my mother. "Oh, like a jackass, I got in the car and drove all the way back. Yes. To Fairlington. Grandma Schultz's. I thought at first, you know, of going into Chambersburg to your uncle Joe and aunt Vee's place. They always make me feel welcome. But Dick, to be honest, I was so crestfallen, I just couldn't handle it. So I drove all the way home."

"Well, Mom," I say, after a long intake of breath, "you deserve better than that."

"Yes I do," she says emphatically. "I certainly do!"

I pause, considering. "I know it's none of my business, but I'm curious. I'll be honest. Where the hell does he get the money to build a fancy house like this?"

It's my mother's turn to pause. I can tell from her silence that my question has thrown her off. "Well," she starts slowly. "Of course, as you know, he inherited money from Grandma Wertime. Sixty-nine thousand dollars. Yes. He's used that, I guess. For the rest, he's had to get a loan from the bank."

"And has he put this on *you*, all these financial dealings? Most of the financial stuff has been on *your* shoulders all these years."

"Oh, no!" she says promptly, with a dry, mirthless chuckle. "Not one bit of it! I made it *very* clear to your father that the house was *his* to finance. I went with him to the bank, though. The local one, in McConnellsburg. He borrowed forty thousand dollars."

"That much. Wow!"

"Well, we do have collateral. Our house and our share of the mountain place. And Grandma Schultz's apartment—though of course we wouldn't *touch* that. No, we own Grandma's place . . ."

The phone drops in its cradle after I've assured my mother that I'll keep in touch with her. I've urged her, as well, to let me know what develops.

I inhale again. My thoughts go back some six months, to October—*You knew there was something he was hiding, didn't you! . . .*

It's a fair day. Bright sunlight. Enough chill in the air to suggest a light jacket. The maples aflame.

Marcia and I are out to visit the site of my father's house, just for the afternoon. We've made the long trip in response to my mother's asking us (*"Your dad would appreciate it so much!"* she'd said. *"Your opinion means a great deal to him, you know that . . ."*), although I'm not really sure what will be expected of us—or entirely sure why we've come.

The bulldozers are snarling and belching dark smoke as we come up the drive. At this point the house doesn't even exist; there's nothing to be seen but a muddy dirt platform heaped against the side of a very steep rock slope. It's atop this platform that the house will stand, eventually.

"Greetings!" says my father as he makes his way toward us. It's hard, at first, to hear him over the din of the equipment. Four local workmen are milling about busily.

He looks weathered. He's wearing a frayed ball cap, an old shirt, muddy corduroys, and heavy workman's boots. What I notice most about him are the deepened etchings around his eyes, the rougher brow, the hair even more silver. Construction work will do that to you. In August he'd turned fifty-seven.

He invites us over to the edge of the platform, urging us, smiling, to enjoy the great view. It *is* that, no question—a vista that opens to the south and east, spilling across the valley to the flank of Tuscarora. Looking south, we see a sweep of blue autumn air coursing over fertile farmlands and the deep green forests that canopy the mountains. Even if the siting of his new house is eccentric—shockingly so, to my mind—the view my father has is splendid.

I turn and smile at him, still deafened by the noise. He shouts things at me that I can't make out—things about

McConnellsburg, the town down in the valley (hard to see through the trees, still); the house, to be constructed of sprayed concrete and steel . . .

Eventually he, Marcia, and I detach ourselves. We find refuge by our car, parked slightly over the crown of the hill.

My father starts afresh. "I'm glad you've come out! You can see how things are starting to shape up already."

In your mind's eye, I think. *In your eyes alone!*

I'm stirred by a memory; there's something familiar, something oddly familiar, about this setup, this whole situation. But the memory doesn't come to me.

My father is ready, now, to get right to the point. He wants me, he says, to hike across his new property with him. It'll take us, very likely, no more than an hour—not *even* an hour. If Marcia is willing to sit here and read, why . . .

We begin by climbing to the top of the huge rock slope. From here to the platform it's a stark, steep drop, and it occurs to me to wonder what it's going to be like, having this waiting landslide poised above his new house. But then I think, *He's building here as a dare to the forces!* One slight tremor, which is perfectly possible, and the result would be chaos. Still, the view from here *is* splendid . . .

A cool autumn breeze blows against our chests and faces. We turn for our hike, my father stepping into the lead.

These acres that he's purchased—160, all told—are not fine woodland. Mainly, they depress me: despite the green mountains that lift all around us, interspersed with valleys rich in fine farms and meadows, he has opted for a stony ridge that slopes on its western side toward swamp and thin tree stands. I can see at a glance, as we tramp along a stream course, that this land won't be yielding any timber soon. Young oaks and hickories; a scattering of maples; here and there fledgling beeches—it's second-cut

growth, the leftovers, mainly, of recent hard logging. Dark hemlocks bunch where the streambed is wettest, and birches and
aspens cover the stretches farther down, where the land runs
into swamp.

My father is decisive now; no waiting around for an agenda to
evolve. "Dick!" he starts in. "I'm interested in having your
responses to those pieces I've published in the *Post*. You got
them, I gather."

"Yes."

"I'd asked Peg to mail them."

"Yes. They came in good order."

"So—what did you think?"

The Washington Post has run two long essays that my father
has written as part of its coverage of the Bicentennial. Printed on
the op-ed page, they ponder the current state of matters in America but bear my father's stamp as a historian of science and
ancient technology. They offer less a thesis than a broad overview,
one that roams across a wide array of subjects—everything from
the Etruscans in the fourth century B.C. to Crèvecoeur's views
on the fledgling United States. The first of these essays appeared
on January 1; the second on July 5, one day after the bicentennial celebration.

"Impressive!" I say. "Very erudite, both of them."

"The response has been good!" my father says as we're walking. "I've had calls and letters."

I say I can imagine so. "I hadn't been aware that the *Post* was
going to publish you! Congratulations!" I pause. "How did this
happen?"

"Why, I prevailed upon Meg Greenfield—"

"Who's . . ."

". . . chief of the editorial page for the *Post*; she's a *very* bright,
very capable, powerful woman. I argued with Meg, whom I met

at a conference, that the paper ought to take a truly visionary look at where the country was headed. She bought the idea! They've already accepted another of my essays, though it may not appear until sometime next year." My father's chin shoves forward. "*That* one, I can promise, is going to turn a few heads! But anyhow. More. More about the first two, and how you responded."

I'm diplomatic with him. The truth is that, for me, his essays are a source of admiration and alarm almost equally mixed; on the one hand, I'm authentically impressed by the ease with which he moves, and moves authoritatively, across so remarkable a body of arcana—early American history as well as all the lore he's mastered in the fields of metallurgy, literature, and social science; on the other hand, I find myself disquieted by his tenor. The titles are part of it: "The Aging of America"; "The New American Revolution." A stridency underlies his stance in each essay; and in both pieces, for me, there's a final lack of focus, lack of a *center* to his argument. Global warming and upheaval; overpopulation; deforestation; the Industrial Revolution; the mixed blessings of technology; the need, as he calls it, for "a New American Maoism in a post-Copernican age," which would involve sending ghetto blacks back down South . . . There are other odd things. Divorce and rising homosexuality, he claims in one of the essays, are telltale symptoms of our national crisis, the falling apart of our old scheme of values. What *they* have to do with deforestation or the Industrial Revolution, I can't quite figure.

But there's much good to emphasize, and I do so willingly. "Dick," he says, "I thank you."

"You're welcome," I say.

"I could wish you equally good fortune in *your* labors."

It's a comment that jolts me. It alludes, if indirectly, to a hard transition I've gone through lately: I'd lost my bid for tenure at Rutgers, where I'd taught for seven years, and have accepted an appointment, at a much-reduced salary, at a small private college in the Philadelphia suburbs. Marcia and I have moved again and are re-establishing ourselves.

I'm about to respond when my father continues. "You remember how I'd mentioned, that night down in Corinth—my fiftieth birthday, not a very easy evening!—that you needn't be wedded to the life of a literary critic? It's my guess that you felt quite offended at the time. Your Ph.D. was fresh, conferred just two months before . . . and I'm sure you didn't want to hear me talk on that occasion about your possibly getting out of academic circles!"

I step over a root as we walk, but say nothing. Still, my head bobs slightly.

"I meant no offense. I would just have you bear in mind that the world's a broad meadow for a person of your talents. You're an uncommon writer, an eloquent person. I know you love teaching."

"I do," I say flatly.

"You know, John and Steve," my father says, changing tack, "have agreed now to collaborate with me on several fronts: working with me at the Smithsonian, maybe an expedition . . . I've secured Steve a position as co-editor—co-author, really!—on one of my upcoming volumes . . ."

"And Charlie?" I say. "How's *he* doing these days?"

"Oh. Charlie—" he says. "Well! Doing better, I think . . . *Quite* well, in his own way. He's on a much better diet of medication now. And I'm doing my damnedest to get him a job up here."

"*Up here?*"

"In the valley. Yes. In a federally funded program. He'd be doing manual labor, home insulation. It'd get him outdoors a lot."

The idea simply stuns me. "So . . . And Steve's editing for you."

"Yes. My new book on tin. As you very well know, he's had a tough time of it since he finished at Chicago."

A Ph.D. in English also, my brother hasn't had any luck in trying to break into the academic marketplace. His wife, Jackie, works for the Red Cross now, while he works toward his real-estate license.

"And Mom, then. How's *she* doing?"

At this, my father stiffens. "Oh, she's down there," he says. "Looking after the home fires. Preoccupied with her matters. Of course, Grandma Schultz is one of the major problems for us."

"Really? How's that?"

My father stares off into the woods. "The old woman is eating up our precious resources! And your mother caters to her in the worst damn way. I hardly see *any* of her! She spends all her time taking care of your grandmother—"

"Well, and of Charlie too, I take it!"

"Yes. That's true. For the moment."

I sense a false note here, but can't quite place it. "I'm sure Mom's concerned about everybody's welfare."

My father turns, eyes glaring. "Dick, that may be! I won't choose to doubt it. The fact remains, however, that the whole family needs to understand what I'm about here. I'm doing my best to create a family base—a material base, yes, with this house that I'm building, but a base in *several* senses—that will sustain us as we move into the difficult times approaching. We've got this election coming up now—this election for President—that absolutely scares the *bejesus* out of me. Why? Because I think this Jimmy Carter has a dictatorial streak. I don't at all trust him, *or* this Ham Jordan fellow. They've managed to move themselves into our national politics with an almost *sinister* cunning! And if you look at Carter's record as governor of Georgia, you'll see in a minute that he's absolutely no friend whatever of civil rights! What he might do with his Joint Chiefs of Staff, once he gets in the White House, constitutes for me a spectacle of frightening proportions!"

He pauses.

"Well! Anyway. Politics aside. As we were saying—"

I choose to say nothing.

It's my father's turn now to drop into silence. His face goes grim, and he looks away from me.

How differently he and I recall that Greek evening, the one in Corinth! What opposite meanings it holds for each of us! His fiftieth birthday . . .

August 31, 1969. It comes back to me as we traverse his sparse woodlands . . .

My father has promised us a lyrical excursion for our last night in Greece: drive down, see the ruins, linger as evening comes in order to celebrate his birthday—a swim in the gulf, then dinner at a *taverna* right there by the water . . . I'm guardedly optimistic; my parents have been at best intermittently hospitable since Marcia and I arrived here for our two-week visit. We'd gone with them to Thessaloniki, but *that* trip ended up being a disaster—a polluted harbor, no swimming (this after my father had promised "the finest swimming in Greece")—and afterward we'd fled by ourselves down to Paros for a few restful days. Still, I'm always hopeful with him that he'll turn things around and make good on his promises.

He doesn't. Not this evening. On our way down to Corinth he drives like a lunatic, his huge station wagon with its diplomatic plates a bully's black weapon as he muscles his way past wary Greek drivers and blasts through the tollbooth when we get to the turnpike. At the ruins—in our company are my father's sister Selma and her three teenage daughters—he is quite beside himself: he shouts at everyone, orders us around, hurries all of us from one spot to another so that none of us can savor the place where Saint Paul preached, or enjoy the scratched line where the Olympic races started, or get more than a hurried glance at the famous museum. He snuffs out objections, makes Selma's girls nervous, disparages my mother, and celebrates his fiftieth with an unending tantrum.

Evening deepens. We drive to the gulf's edge.

Marcia and I escape to the beach for a swim, where we're joined by my mother. When I comment on how boorish my father is being, she grows tolerant, forgiving. "Well, be patient," she says. "You know it's his birthday."

I'm unpersuaded.

We return to the *taverna* to find my father fully manic. He's all joviality now. He calls for the musicians, pretending to be Zorba; spins the girls around the dance floor, despite their protests and giggles. Barks orders to the waiters, who take less kindly to his tone than he imagines.

I've finally had enough when he makes his approach to me. He's genial, smiling. "Well! Now that you've finally gotten your Ph.D.," he says, "we have to work to get you out of academic life!"

"'Out of academic life'?" I say. "What does that mean?"

"Well," he says, his jaw rotating, "it's all well and good to have such impressive credentials, but you need *experience* now."

I ask, "What kind?"

"Well." He pauses. "Of the broader sort."

"Why," I say, smiling. "I thought that that was more or less what I was getting out here."

He looks down at the table. Then his eyes lift to me. It's time for him to be bold now. "Well, frankly I was hoping that you would come work for *me*. You know, John and Steve have already agreed—"

I interrupt. "Doing what?"

"Why, research!" he answers.

"*Sure*. I do that already."

"But the fine-grained work they have you doing in academe—"

"Wait. Hold it a moment. We needn't get into that!" I'm piloting the boat toward the edge of the drop now. "You said that you wanted me to come work for you. So—what do you offer?"

"Offer?"

"Yes! Your *terms*."

He goes blank. Silent.

"There have to be *terms*! I have a job. A salary. Benefits! So I'd need to know what *terms* you'd be able to match. I'm an assistant professor at a big research university! I repeat, then: *What's your offer?*"

My father is in retreat now; the dark oil of shame has started to leak from his being. I'm cruel in my insistence. I'm factual. Cheerful. Easy. I'm not going to let him off the hook lightly now; the sentence must stick. As we confer, I watch my father descend a long ladder toward some drab inner cellar where his musty hopes are stored; watch him tally his futilities, watch him count the heaped errors. For once I'm in control; it's mine to mete out the punishment.

I don't spare the rod.

ROOFTOP

What will it be like, this new house of my father's?

We discuss it, Marcia and I, as we thread down the valley. We've taken the turnpike as far as Fort Littleton, then picked up Route 522 toward McConnellsburg. Traffic's light; it's Thanksgiving. A fair day. Warm enough out. Puffed, fleecy clouds occasionally dropping cool shadows.

"Well" I say, "at least we won't have this Joan of his to deal with."

"I wonder how your mother puts up with it," says Marcia.

"Beats me. But he's promised."

"Grandma Schultz will be there?"

"Yes."

We've driven a dozen miles through the troughlike low valley that anchors the mountains. Tuscarora's blue hump rises on

our left, but my eye's to the right, playing the ridge top. Its tree line dips and lifts, showing sudden bald patches—scree slopes, exactly what my eye is looking for. I scan them, disappointed.

Then suddenly I see it, floating up there like an ark. It's brilliant through the trees, a white bird perched on top of the mountain. "There it is!" I say to Marcia.

She cranes her neck. "You're sure?"

"Well, yes!" I answer. "That has got to be it." I point. "To the left there! Where the road goes over the mountain. Can you see?"

We're both excited.

McConnellsburg's asleep. We drift in on its east side into the quiet town square. The town hall is a brick building with white window sashes and tall Doric columns. A Methodist church commands the square's northwest corner.

Most of the town is strung along the Lincoln Highway, old Route 30. Again I'm impressed by the absence of life here: we make up the traffic. A reddish grit has sifted across the gutters and sidewalks. The feel, oddly enough, is of a cow town out West.

We turn right. The road climbs into brown-stubbled corn-fields less than half a mile out. The new bypass glistens in its concrete on our right side, but we take the old road, whose macadam is lichened with darkened seams and patchy breaks, like the back of some beast. Hemlocks shade the sharper turns. Winds stunt the oaks here. A white birch flashes.

At the top, we come to my father's driveway almost immediately. It's a steep, harrowing incline sliced from raw shale, and the roadside embankment here looks like carved ham. I hit the gas hard. Our car tilts skyward; the gears groan and whine, our tires spitting shale. After a hundred yards of thrashing and scary fishtailing, we make it to the top.

"That's some driveway," Marcia mutters.

"It's no better. That's for sure."

But my focus is elsewhere. The last time we'd been here, we'd seen nothing but a flat, dull platform of dirt, a scattering of work-men, and the loud bulldozers. Now, a house! As if by magic — the snapping of the fingers of some airborne giant. It looks like a Greek church snatched from its moorings on some Cycladic island, hand-molded, almost, with its rounded corners and edges. Its whitewash is brilliant.

Newness typifies everything here. Felled trees lie aslant where my father is working to create a clearing on the sunny southern side of the house, and construction debris—wire mesh, mangled lumber, the white plastic buckets that joint compound comes in—litters the fringes of the cramped space for cars.

I park. We get out. I take a deep breath, girding myself for what's to follow. But there are no other cars here.

Puzzled, we enter.

I shout up the stairway. The main living space is on the second, not the ground, floor, though there's also a ground-level hall we could follow. When we get no answer, we go ahead and climb the stairs, our footfalls muffled by the deep gold carpeting.

At the top, we turn right and go down a short hall.

We step into a light-bathed chamber large enough to let our vision take flight. A sparrow released here could soar into freedom before deciding where to perch. Filigreed lamps hang on long copper chains from the high, vaulted ceiling; a stained-glass window spreads its bright, varied colors at the far end of the space . . .

But the light! It cascades here. It pours its abundance. There are palm trees, philodendrons, a glistening walnut table, Persian carpets sprawling like great lazy cats soaking up the autumn sun . . .

Marcia reaches over and presses her fingers into my biceps. "It's beautiful," she murmurs.

We step forward carefully, two people entering an almost-forbidden garden.

A voice calls my name from what seems a great height. I stop, alarmed.

I turn to my right to discover—

"Grandma Schultz!" I say. Her name comes out loudly. I can't help laughing.

We greet my grandmother.

Grandma Schultz is wearing a dark navy dress, gold button earrings, and a simple string of pearls. She has her high heels on and has put her false teeth in. Her hair is freshly done, though the beautician's rinse has tinted it a shade too purple. She looks elegant, formal. She's eighty-two now.

"I didn't hear you come in," she says. She walks forward from an area that I see, now, is the kitchen. It's accommodating, open, with south-facing windows.

"So, where *is* everybody?"

My grandmother—nothing if not direct—shakes her head. "Dick, your parents are off somewhere. Doing what? Don't ask me. They're always *scheissing* around, those two! I've never seen a tribe that was so full of commotion!"

I laugh again. "At first it seemed like no one was here."

"Oh, the whole gang is coming. Steve and Jackie and their boy. John. *His* whole crew. Charlie. But"—my grandmother pauses—"we're not ready for you yet!"

I pause at this, puzzled. "Are we *that* early? Jeez."

"Dinner won't be till two. You should come back at one."

My watch says noon.

Come back?

I'm speechless.

I glance over at Marcia. She's as nonplussed as I am.

"Well, okay," I say.

As we drift down the mountain, a laugh exits from me. "Good Christ! What a welcome!"

Marcia isn't any more pleased than I am, but her tone is more forgiving. "There's your grandmother, cooking! I must say, it smelled delicious. It looks like she's doing the whole dinner by herself."

"I'm hungry. How about you?"

"Yes."

I propose we look for something. "Though around *these* parts . . ."

McConnellsburg has settled deeper into its holiday stupor. We prowl the main drag, reading the braille of shut-up buildings: an H&R Block office, a deli, a beautician's shop, a deserted Amoco station. There are two historic buildings: the Fulton House, dating from 1793, a handsome limestone inn with a wood-plank porch; and an early stone-fronted house that is now a dentist's office. Both are tightly shuttered.

At the far edge of town we come upon a Sheetz, a new gas station–minimart complex. We buy Coke and chocolate milk and one wrapped hoagie, which we split in the car. I comment to Marcia how strange it seems to me that my father would have picked *this* town, of all places, to build his retirement home—a town we have no connection to whatsoever . . .

It's exactly one o'clock when we get back up the mountain. My parents' big sedan is parked beneath the hickories.

By the time we've unbelted, my father has appeared. He's dressed in gray slacks and a white turtleneck, his hair neatly trimmed; he's looking more healthy and distinctly more youthful than the last time we saw him, over a year ago now.

He approaches us, smiling. But something alerts me—the hunch of his shoulders, the lift of his eyebrows.

"Greetings!" he says to us, and steps forward to hug my wife. His handshake is firm.

I feel a strong impulse to say something, but he has already started. "Ah, listen," he begins. "You remember what we said when we were having that conversation? Well . . ."

He pauses.

I wait.

Marcia, of course, is here, standing right next to me. But he and I are alone now. The world strips away, and he and I confront each other on a windy promontory, pines in the background, miles of dark slate sliding off into the sky.

Goddammit, you promised us! my heart is busy saying. *That was the deal—no Joan here today! You gave your solemn word on it.*

"So," he says, his mouth twisted . . .

Of course. Joan's here.

The news sends me plunging.

When I refocus on him, he's in the middle of his sentence: ". . . and she's in need of help now, you see; she's alone in the world . . ."

Rendered mute, I hear nothing. But my sense of sight is sharpened. In the glass of my deafness, I see a man groveling, a face all contorted, a parody of the wretched hangdog lover in disgrace—*Herr Professor, I smell garbage . . .*

And then he's concluding, though his eye won't meet mine: "So you see . . ." He asks for our patience. Hopes for our understanding.

As if he really needs it.

What can one do if people act in bad faith?

"Well. We're here," I answer simply.

And exhale. It's over.

My father, cheered, is ready to go about his business now. Expansively, he invites us into the house for a look around.

We climb the stairs. My mother greets us. An awkwardness ensues as we explain that in fact we'd been here earlier.

"What? Grandma sent you *away*?" My mother's laughter mixes mortification with amusement. "Marcia and Dick! I'm so sorry. She shouldn't have done that!"

"Well," I say, "she was busy. No harm done."

We re-greet my grandmother, who is wearing an apron now. I wonder when my brothers are going to get here. And Joan—what about her?

These concerns have to wait. We step, at last, fully into the open living room, whose layout now is clearer. The dining and living areas make one great open chamber under the barrel-vaulted ceiling, which lifts to a height of eighteen feet at its apex. The kitchen, shaped like a half-moon, is adjacent to the dining area. There's no partition. The whole expanse, then, creates a single fluid space, undivided and coherent. A chandelier hangs over the big dining table.

I'm drawn at once, mothlike, to the floor-to-ceiling windows along the room's southern side. What a prospect spreads before me! It's as if a light airplane has lifted me up into the cloud deck and allowed me to peer down on a spread hand of mountains. Startled by the thousand-foot dropoff at my feet, I step back for an instant.

My father appears next to my elbow, excited. "Isn't that a *view*? You can see almost all the way to Hancock, Maryland. A full thirty miles!"

Marcia comes over, touching my other arm lightly. "Ted, it's just lovely."

Farms and silos. Barns glinting. A quilt of brown cornfields. It's a seesaw valley, clasped between two mountains.

My father, in his element now, starts to lecture. "This house is a work of sheer genius, I'll tell you! A marvel of engineering! All the windows face south to take advantage of the sunlight—why, it's so absolutely energy-efficient that I can heat the whole place with just a couple of logs! *If* I have to use the wood-stove. And once the solar panels on the roof are working right—I've got adjustments to make there—we won't even need that! We miss all the wind. The boulders in back of the house give protection. If you climb to the top of the ridge on a windy day, the temperature drops twenty degrees in an instant!"

My father pauses here. "I'd hired at first, you know, this bright young architect to help me with this place. A very talented, pleasant fellow. But it was the goddamnedest thing! He just couldn't grasp the essential principles of it all! He kept submitting plans that had these small, narrow windows and this huddled-in feeling. So finally I fired him. By God, I fired him!" My father's jaw works.

My wife and I trade glances, but he doesn't notice.

"Then I fired another architect! And another after that! It took me *four architects* to get this place built! I finally found a man from over near Saint Thomas to give me a hand. Bob Scott is his name. Bob was worth all the others I'd hired put together! He could grasp what I was doing. And by God, I needed him! We went through the tortures of the damned to build this place. When we started spraying concrete—the very first layer—the frame began to sag. The weight was too great. We had to get a well-digging rig up in here to drop shafts down *thirty feet*. We filled them with reinforced steel and cement to bolster the foot-ings. And then—"

Suddenly Charlie enters. He strides into the living room and greets me and Marcia, his blond hair flying and his face visibly windburned. It looks as if he's been out in the sun for hours, though his face could be weathered from the job he's recently started, doing home insulation here in the valley.

I shake his hand. "You've been busy!"

My comment subdues him; he pauses, struggles with it. "Oh, yeah," he says finally. "I've been helping somebody. Mom and Dad, uh, have this older friend, Helen. She lives down the valley . . ."

My mother has come in now and stands behind Charlie. "I'm sure you'd both love her. Eighty years old and she drives like the dickens! She owns this big Cadillac —"

My father interrupts. "Charlie! You didn't let the dog in, did you?"

Charlie's not sure. "I'll go check," he offers.

"Please do," my father says, and looks squarely at my brother with a challenging expression.

Charlie turns toward the stairway.

Till now, I've just listened. "A *dog*?" I say, smiling.

"Why, yes!" says my father. "Come have a look! I'm sure you'll both like her."

We follow my father back down the carpeted stairway and out the front door. He leads us around to the northern side of the house, which lies in the shadows. Tucked out of the way, at the foot of the sloping boulders, stands a small wooden doghouse. At first it seems empty. My father kneels, reaches in, and roughly drags the dog out. She's a timid young female, a low-slung, long-eared beagle. When she sees us two strangers, she squats down, thumps her short white tail, and averts her head, as if she suddenly fears something.

"This is Gretta," says my father.

As soon as his hand nears her, her tail thumps even harder and her whole body trembles. We ask if she's friendly.

My father doesn't answer us—at least not directly. He starts to explain how they'd come to be her owners. She'd been rescued from a lab that was being shut down by the local authorities. When my father first got her, she was thin from starvation and traumatized by the experiments that had been done on her. "Look," he says. "She has a tattoo in her ear." He lifts the flap to show us five blue digits. He adds matter-of-factly, as he pulls himself upright, "I call her my Jew-dog." Stunned, Marcia and I swap looks. "She's still quite timid."

"I notice," I say, "that she didn't bark when we first got here."

"She *doesn't* bark," my father answers. "She isn't much of a watchdog."

My wife and I kneel and put our hands out to Gretta. At our touch she starts to tremble, as she did with my father, and her head turns sideways till the whites of her eyes show. She's an unhandsome dog, more like a dachshund than a beagle—too pale, too long to be a purebred—but her fur is soft and silky. We speak gentle words. The trembling continues, but her tail thumps softly.

"Let's go back in," my father says shortly. He has more to tell and show us.

At the top of the stairs, my mother is waiting. She's dressed in a floral print dress that seems springlike. "Marcia and Dick!" she exclaims. "Let me show you Grandma's bedroom."

My father growls at her. "Well, Peg, make it quick!"

"Jeepers, Ted. What's the rush?"

"We need time to talk."

"This'll only take a minute!"

My father goes ahead, diverted, it seems, by other business. I'm perplexed by this exchange but say nothing, an old habit.

We turn to the left, down a very short hallway. "Isn't Gretta sweet?" says my mother, as she walks ahead of us. She doesn't wait for an answer. "It's *so* nice of you to come all this distance. And Marcia, you look lovely! . . . It's a fine house, isn't it? Your father did a wonderful job. Here, now. This is Grandma's bedroom."

We step into a chamber not much more than ten feet square. "It's modest!" I murmur.

My mother's voice dips here. "Your father, you know, wanted to make it even smaller, but I finally said to him, 'Ted, that wouldn't be fair.'" Again she shifts subjects. "I'm sorry, by the way—no, that's not the right word; *appalled* would be better—that Grandma didn't invite you to stay when you first got here. I can't imagine what was in her mind when she did that!"

A short laugh follows this admission of disbelief, though I can tell that my mother is authentically embarrassed.

"Well," I say, my tone congenial, "she was probably nervous."

"She *is*," admits my mother, "doing the whole Thanksgiving dinner. I must say, I'm grateful to her. She's been a big help."

"And you to her," I answer.

My mother takes a sudden step closer to us, her head inclined slightly. She looks over her shoulder, as if someone might hear her. She says, in a whisper, "You know that Joan's here, don't you?"

Marcia and I both nod.

"Well, she's down in our big bedroom. Let me go introduce you."

My shoes root themselves to the pile of the carpet. So this is how the matter is finally to be broached.

It strikes me, for the first time, how quiet and observant, how carefully unobtrusive Marcia has been. Clearly, she has paid more attention than I have. I say to my mother, as if nothing's at issue, "You know, we haven't even seen the lower part of the house yet!"

"Oh, you *haven't?*" Her voice is musical. "Well, then, let me show you!"

Carpeted stairs lead from the dining area to the ground floor. We seem to be descending into the cellar of some fortress where the wine is kept. We glimpse a wide bedroom half encircled by full-length windows—again the great view; it's the second-largest bedroom—while my mother explains to us one of the house's odder features. Along the hall that runs to my parents' bedroom are a pair of indentations, like the molds for broad, half-rounded columns; these bays let the warm air rise to the upper part of the house. There are two such bays in the hallway and one in their bedroom.

My mother pauses.

"I should tell you," she says, her voice again dipping, "that Joan is a person who can be quite temperamental. She's not very well. She has good qualities, but you don't always see them. So don't be surprised if she seems a bit frightful."

I'm glad for the warning.

The apparition that greets us in the bedroom shocks me. My father's latest mistress is a gaunt, black-haired woman, so visibly anorexic that her legs are like spindles; she sways when she

greets us. Her eyes are cavernous, angry. Her voice is as low, as much like a man's, as my mother had said it was.

It's an uncomfortable encounter. The bedroom is dominated by an oversized bed with a rich blue coverlet and a high mattress. An upholstered chair sits across the room, by the windows — sliding doors, really; they issue onto a margin of grassed-over earth before the dropoff begins. It's a spare room, although the carpet is a luxuriant Oriental. There are drapes. A pair of dressers. No other chairs to sit on. A woodstove sits in the bay along the north wall. Today it's unlit.

Our brief meeting over, we take our leave of Joan and make our way back upstairs. I don't believe I've spoken more than twenty words to her.

Up in the living area, my father is waiting for us. He makes no acknowledgment that we've just met his mistress, this woman so at odds with my blond, cheery mother. He wants me, he says, to go back outdoors with him to have a look at a couple of things before the rest of the family gets here.

I tell Marcia we'll return soon and follow him outside. The clouds have cleared away, and a light breeze is blowing. I take a deep breath, relieved for the moment to be outdoors again. The sun is benign, surprisingly bright for this season. It reflects off the stuccolike concrete of the house with an eye-pinching brilliance. Rich smells from the woods put a tang in the air.

First, my father says, he'd like to show me his swimming pool. I'm incredulous at first, having heard nothing of this. He leads me along the southern wall of the house, where the sun is the brightest and the dropoff the steepest.

This brings us out, finally, on the easternmost side. Here a rough basin has been gouged into the rock slope, an irregular depression maybe twenty feet across and five feet deep. It's coated over thinly with a layer of cement. A veneer of brackish water is puddled in its deepest part.

I almost laugh, but catch myself. A swimming pool! Jesus.

"It's going to take some work yet," my father says, musing. His eyebrows lift.

I can't think of anything to say in response, so I listen while my father describes his intentions. He'll capture some of the water in the form of natural runoff; he'll use well water, too . . . Politely, I nod. What strikes me as I listen is that a *real* swimming pool, built by a qualified builder, complete with a deck that took advantage of this vista, would constitute a spectacular addition to the place.

"The other thing I wanted to show you," he says when he's finished, "are my ingenious solar panels! They're up on the roof."

The roof! Good lord.

I shrug. Well, I guess I'm no stranger to roofs. "Where's your ladder?"

"Over here."

As we continue around the house, he says, "Oh, by the way, I wanted to ask you. Did you read my third essay in *The Washington Post*? It came out in April."

It pains me to admit it: "To be honest, I haven't. Marcia and I have been so busy—"

"I hope you will!" he says. "I raise the question of whether we've come to the end of the world's golden age. It's provocative, I assure you. But it's nothing compared to my next piece for the *Post*, which I'm working on now. It'll deliver quite a bombshell."

"How's that?" I say, pausing.

"I'm proposing," my father says, his head tilted back, "that we start to think seriously of underground housing."

"Underground—?"

"Housing. Yes."

I can think of nothing to say.

"There's much to be said, in terms of energy conservation and the protection of the environment, for putting our houses *under* the soil. Canyon dwellers out West, in fact, are doing it already—a return, of a sort, to the old prairie practice of building houses out of sod or tucking them into embankments."

"As in Willa Cather, say."

My father stares at me.

Embarrassed, I explain. "You find houses like that in a couple of her novels. *O Pioneers! My Ántonia.* They're set in Nebraska—"

"Of course!" says my father. "I know Cather well!"

My eyes drop.

He goes on, his voice brisk. "I'm thinking, now, of starting up an energy consortium. Yes! An energy consortium. We'd promote the new technologies and the innovative strategies I've set forth in the *Post.* There exist now, you see, all these exquisite small technologies—wind and solar power devices; water conservation methods—that can drastically cut pollution and help us save the environment. It's eroding at a pace now that few people fathom. The grasses are dying in the highlands of Colombia as a result of global warming, and great tracts of the planet are reverting to desert. It's a very real crisis. The permafrost is starting to collapse in the Arctic Circle, with God only knows what dire eventual consequences . . . And yet, you see, it isn't hopeless." His eyes grow bright. "It isn't at *all* hopeless! That's what I've argued in the *Post.* Our technological power is immense at this point—*if* we use it for good! *If* we manage to wean ourselves from dreadful things like nuclear power, utter folly and destruction, given the half-life—*eons!*—of our nuclear pollutants. *The Washington Star* did an interview with me—this was back in February—in which I set forth some key steps for heading off the great calamity that awaits us if we don't get our lives in serious order."

My father takes a breath here. "I made a pilgrimage, you know, to see Scott and Helen Nearing at their farm up in Maine. They're the authors of a book called *Living the Good Life.* They've become central figures in the self-sufficiency movement. We had quite a meeting! The three of us discussed the world's challenges for *hours*, sitting out there by their organic garden, which is truly a wonder . . . But the key is education. Education! Getting the word out. It takes the right voice to make these things *heard* by people. They require an eloquent spokesman."

He fixes his gaze on me. "*That*, you see, was one of the things I thought might interest you, given your talents as a writer. When I write my pieces for *The Washington Post*, I craft my best prose, since the audience is a good one—but I lack your flair."

"You do fine," I say flatly.

"You're very kind."

"Not at all."

"Well!" he says. He ceases.

We've reached the north side of the house, and the ladder.

"Watch your step," my father warns. "There's a slightly loose rung about halfway up."

I need no coaching. As I plant my foot on the first rung, I inhale quickly and remind myself again that the best way to climb is to look straight ahead, neither up nor down. My nerves have steadied by the time we've reached the top.

The rooftop is a black expanse, humped in the middle where the barrel-vaulted ceiling rises to its apex. Its tarred finish is rough. My father has done some patching where his big solar panels have created minor problems, but once they're fully functional, they'll give, he says, abundant heat.

A gust catches my shirt and momentarily unsteadies me. I take a few steps to regain my footing. My hand comes up to shield my eyes against the sun. "What a view!" I exclaim.

My vision sweeps the valley, the mountains, the farmlands.

"Isn't it!" says my father. "You know, one of the things we most enjoy about this house is the music we can make here."

"I'll bet," I say, smiling.

"The acoustics in the living room are absolutely perfect. To be playing string quartets with this view in the background—it's

nearly paradisal. I've enticed Phil Jones, you know, and all the old gang to come up here to play. We did the Brahms Quintet recently. And two of the great Schubert pieces."

"I wish I could have heard you!"

"I believe Kent enjoyed it."

I turn and stare at my father. "What? My son? Kent?"

"Why, yes!" he says. He pauses. "Kent was here for the weekend."

I laugh in astonishment. "*I didn't know that!*"

"Indeed!" says my father, trying to sound matter-of-fact. "He's been here several times. I'd recruited him, in fact, to do some good, heavy labor. He and Charlie teamed up to give me a hand one weekend. I set those boys to loading river stones for about twelve hours into the big concrete cistern that the heat pump feeds into! That, you see, is where the heat goes from these solar panels." He smiles in amusement. "The two of them slept well *that* night.

"He's a fine boy, your son," my father continues. "I've drawn him into the fold here because I saw that he needed something that he couldn't get from Jane. A 'broader nurturance,' you might say. A chance to exploit his vigor. Your mother's very fond of Kent! Joan is too, you know."

My legs go bloodless, and the power of speech deserts me for a couple of seconds. "Yes, but—" I say, and then halt. I find my voice, finally. "It wouldn't be a bad idea for *me* to know these things. Not that I object, really . . ."

The betrayals are mounting up so fast I can't count them.

In a sense, I take my leave from here, right from this rooftop. My brothers will assemble, and I'll be glad to see them with their wives, their young sons; my father will talk rather strangely, over dinner, about his new "broadened" family; Grandma Schultz will criticize poor Charlie for his habits—the worst of her *own* habits; and in the end, somewhat furtively, my mother will press a twenty-dollar bill into my hand, "for expenses," as she'll put it.

But I'm already gone, my mind taking wing. I have plenty to digest, to put to rights in my thinking—Joan at our table, largely silent, her eyes steady; the question of how my mother fits into this with her charity, her complicity; this fresh, bizarre news about Kent's coming up here; my father's intentions . . .

Driving home in the afternoon, I'm suddenly taken by a memory.

It's summer, late '40s. We're spending our vacation in a rented cabin at Cowans Gap; the purchase of the mountain place is three years away still. I'm seven. It's mid-August. My grandfather has just had another heart attack at his home in Pasadena, so my mother's in California to be with her parents, leaving me and my brothers in my father's loose care.

During the month she's gone, my father grows a beard, smokes cigars with the men who visit us (a couple of my uncles), and cooks haphazardly. Every day, for lunch, he makes us a lettuce-and-tuna-fish sandwich generously spread with Miracle Whip. He's accidentally bought this instead of mayonnaise, but having blundered in his purchase, refuses to correct it. He gives us each a dime to get an ice-cream sandwich at the concession stand by the beach.

Then he goes off hiking until late afternoon. I fish in the lake, using the bread in my sandwich to entice the wary bluegills. John and Steve most often spend their day on the beach. Around five-thirty, my father comes down out of the mountains, his face deeply burnished by the sun, his brow gleaming. He always carries with him a big forked stick whose lower end bears strike marks, vivid green stains where the rattlers and copperheads have struck it as he's pinned them. One day I ask him to bring me some rattles. When he complies, I grieve deeply that I've cost the snake its life and have visions of it squirming, its neck pinned solidly beneath the forked stick.

My father returns early from his hike one evening and invites all of us to climb a nearby low mountain. It's the mountain that looks to the east, out over the lake. At the top we discover a simple, sturdy wooden structure—a Geological Survey tower. We climb its vertical ladder, rung over rung, and come out on a platform surrounded by a railing. My father directs our gaze toward the shining northwest. There, to our amazement, the noses of two mountains come down and touch.

"The Alligators," my father says.

Indeed, these two mountains do resemble alligators, even in the manner in which the patches of farm and forest seem to give them shortened forelegs. For their eyes, gray scree slopes. Their backs curve up toward us.

. . . And this has come back now, while we drive toward Philadelphia, because—how can it be?—the left-hand alligator is where my father's new house sits. The road from Fort Little-ton, the one from the turnpike, runs through the gap.

Where the giant noses touch.

How, I'm asking myself, *does he get so much power?*

For it's clear to me, clear, that he has cowed my grandmother, for all that she hates him; has tamed the lot of us—my grandmother, my mother, my brothers, and not least, me. *"I play by my own rules. I do no one's bidding."*

Is any of this *planned*? If so, how much?

The day has left me exhausted.

FOUR

A SUDDEN DARKENING

Months pass during which we have no contact with my family. Then the phone rings. It's my father. He says he's very eager to "share the latest developments with us"—whatever they may be. I offer excuses by saying how busy we are. He persists, however, and finally we agree to make a fast trip out to see them. Marcia isn't happy, but she's not unhappy, either: we have news of our own we might choose to share with them.

We leave for McConnellsburg on a Saturday in March. The snow has melted and most of the valleys are turning green, but it's a raw, unpleasant morning at the end of a bad winter. The wind shoves the clouds back and forth across the sky so that the land goes dim and then abruptly reignites as the sun wins its space back.

. . .

I'm expecting, as we fight our way up the steep driveway, that my father will have started to get his place in order. A glance around, however—the driveway is mud, a thick soup at this season—shows me he hasn't. Our eyes are assaulted by the piles of broken lumber, the buckets, the wire mesh, the downed trees lying helter-skelter all about, the whole drab array rendered sooty and dirty-looking by the rigors of winter.

But Gretta has had puppies! What an odd coincidence, given the news that we carry. As we step out of the car at the top of the drive, we're surrounded at the ankles by a happy commotion—winsome, woolly creatures ranging in color from black to amber. Six all told, they haven't quite been weaned. Gretta hovers nearby. She's diffident as usual and thin from all the nursing. But proud, it seems. Proud.

Marcia and I each pick up a pup. Their fur is so rich and fleecy that I say to my father, "So. Who's the dad?"

"You'll see! Come on in."

No sooner have we taken off our coats indoors than my father smiles, explaining, "We all went skating."

"Skating?"

He grins. "You remember that pond where we used to go skating when you boys were still little? The one right in front of the old Heinz factory?"

"Sure. In Chambersburg. Right?"

"Well, we went skating there. During the January cold snap. Joe and Vee came with us."

"—And Gretta met a fellow," my mother chimes in.

Puzzled, I look at them.

"I had my camera," says my father.

Even as he's saying this, my mother is opening a thick photo envelope. She hands the photos to us.

Marcia, not speaking, is right at my elbow, glancing at the pictures as I quickly shuffle through them. There, in the background of almost every picture, is the hulking presence of the old Heinz factory, which on late-summer nights used to cook up ketchup, the pungent odor of spices and tomatoes fragrancing the air. A grim brick structure, no ketchup cooking now, the factory looms up like a penitentiary behind the wintry white foreground where Gretta is being mounted. The sire of her pups is a handsome, strapping Airedale, a full-blooded dog with the rich, crisp fur he's passed on to his offspring. The middle distance holds skaters who might have been stolen from a Brueghel winter landscape, men, women, children, making loops and happy circles.

Gretta is not happy. She stands on the ice, the Airedale's forepaws planted squarely on her back. The whites of her eyes show. She looks at the camera, but her head hangs sideways.

My father guffaws. "She looks as though she's taking it—poor critter—in the ass! Lord! What a *woeful* hound's expression!"

My mother's eyes are squinting, she's laughing so hard. "Oh, and *this*, folks! Look at *this* one! . . ." I feel uneasy as I hand the pictures back. My father and mother are so deep in their merriment they don't even notice our solemn reaction. There must be twenty-four pictures all told, all of Gretta being mounted. A whole roll of film.

I take a deep breath and go ahead and tell them anyway: Marcia and I are trying to start a family now, but we've encountered difficulties. We've been to a number of specialists; the jury's still out on what the exact problem is . . . Our other news is that Marcia has been admitted to the Bryn Mawr School of Social Work.

My parents nod politely. They're not inclined to probe much.

After an extended moment of silence, my father says, "So! Time to share with you the latest on the energy front! It's one of the reasons I wanted to see you."

"Okay." I smile.

My mother, rising from the sofa, invites Marcia down to the big bedroom with her so that they can look at jewelry and clothing together.

"You'll recall," my father begins, scarcely glancing at the women as they make their departure, "that I'd talked with you last fall about my energy consortium. Well, it's off the ground, finally! And then, with Bob Scott's help and the support of a local teacher, I've also launched a technology club at one of the high schools in the valley. Yes. James Buchanan High, just outside of Mercersburg. It's a very bold notion—engaging young people in the conservation effort; introducing them to the very latest technologies for energy hoarding . . . But the *real* stroke of genius is to get them involved in putting the word out to others. We've had one major technology fair already and are planning several others."

"Windmills and things?"

"Those, of course!" says my father. "But we go well beyond that. I'm trying to teach these kids, you see, a concept of technology that is truly comprehensive. It's not just *technē*—constructed things—we deal with. It's *attitudes*. Habits. Expectations for the future. For Christ's sake, even *diet!*—Did you know that how we humans grow the foods we eat, for example, constitutes the planet's most damaging technology? Joan and I, you know"—a quick pause here, then a hurry-up beat—"have embarked on a series of experiments with new crops and foods in a garden down the hillside. Perhaps you and I can have a look at it later. It's revolutionary farming! We started last spring. There are new strains out of the old fruits and vegetables—"

Here my father halts suddenly, breaking off his own story. "Anyhow, Bud Shuster, our local congressman, got word of what we were doing and helped us win a grant to take our project down to Washington. To Capitol Hill! Yes. We set up a display in the Capitol building. It turned out to be quite a feather in Bud's cap."

"Wow," I say. "I'm impressed!"

"You should be!" he says. "Several of the senators sent their staff over, and Ted Kennedy himself came by for a look! He was very impressed with all the displays the kids had built, and talked most knowledgeably about energy conservation. Oh, we had a good crowd! Kennedy came up to me as our program was ending and said, 'Keep it up, Wertime!' He said he thought that we were really on to something."

I'm impressed once again.

"Now," my father says more slowly, "the commercial side of it hasn't gone quite so well. I've solicited John and Steve to undertake the venture with me, though it's unclear whether they'll participate or not. Our plan is to hire ourselves out as consultants, checking houses for leaks—a kind of energy inventory— but it's taking us time. I've even," he adds, "made a brief trip abroad in order to sell the idea. Had brochures printed up— handsome ones, I must say. I made stops out in Greece and Turkey and Iran, at the embassies there. I secured some interest. But we need real capital to invest."

My wife and my mother have returned from their adventure. "I heard you telling Dick about your plans for the consortium," my mother says.

I nod.

"You should have seen the brochures your dad had printed up! They were excellent. Very professional. I'm sure that your father is going to generate some business."

"Well, Peg. We'll see."

My father and I walk around outside for about twenty minutes before Marcia and I leave. He has made some "improvements" he wants to show me. The first is an outhouse he's had put in. It stands fifteen feet from the house's southwest corner, at the base of the rock slope. It'll save, he says, on water. I'm reminded of Grandma Wertime's outhouse, with its dankness and spiders and old *Reader's Digests*.

His second improvement is a fish pond, sort of, a crude irregular trough about ten feet in length and maybe four feet across. It's situated close—oddly close—to the outhouse, adjacent to the place where we usually park our cars. I'd glanced at it while coming in but, distracted by the dogs, had paid it no attention. A foot at its deepest, it's lined with rough cement like his would-be swimming pool—seems, in fact, almost to be a miniature of it. A layer of dead leaves coats the floor of this fish pond, in whose murky, brackish water a few listless goldfish linger. He'll restock it, he says, when the weather gets warm.

Finally, he intends to have a tractor shed built above the garden that he's started. He points down a slope through the stand of bare trees to a slightly leveled area. What has caught my eye, though, are the mounds of trash and garbage that are scattered through the woods here; my father says he's composting, but it looks to me as though he has dispensed with trash removal. One of these trash piles stands close to the front door.

And yet the inside of the house always looks so immaculate! The whole thing's a mystery.

"That garden I was mentioning lies just down the hill. It's a bit too muddy for us to go down there now." We turn back toward the house, but it's clear that my father doesn't want to go in yet. Whatever is on his mind seems to weigh him down. "Your mother," he says, halting, "is drinking quite a lot now. I don't know if you knew that."

"What? *Drinking?*"

"Yes."

"Golly, no! When did *that* start?"

My father is unaware that I've even asked a question. "It *transforms* the woman, Dick. One minute she's her usual self, pleasant and cheery, and the next she's this stiff-faced, red-cheeked, angry creature! She can't handle liquor. Between her and Joan—who, you know, is a heavy drinker—I sometimes have my hands full!"

Much more than you know! I think. But I choose to say nothing. Instead, I ask my father, "What is she drinking?"

"Oh, gin. Wine. Whatever. All I know is the dreadful effect it has on her. I've tried banning liquor altogether from the house, for *both* of the women. But it just doesn't work."

"Well, maybe . . . ," I say. Then I start my sentence over. "It must be a consequence of some kind of stress."

My father looks straight at me. He has missed my point, I think.

"I guess," I add, "you should try to help her stop."

"Mmn. Yes. Perhaps a program."

To this I say nothing.

"And you know, she gets flirtatious—with *Charlie*, for Christ's sake—when she gets liquored up! All giggly and pawing. She used to get that way out in Greece with him sometimes. Christ! I'd have to step in and almost act as a referee!"

YOU sure as hell know how to referee, I think.

. . .

A couple of months later, this letter arrives from him.

Dear Dick:

Meg Greenfield has rejected the latest of the essays that I'd written for the *Post*. She's been polite about it, but it's a blow nonetheless.

This grieves me, I must tell you. I'd written (if I do permit myself to say it plainly) with verve and élan about the impending world crisis; to have this piece declined is effectively to be silenced on a matter about which I have the clearest possible eyesight. We face as a nation—even more, as a planet—a sudden darkening at this hour that few people grasp. I happen to be one of them, not because of any striking wisdom on my part, but because my work affords me a vantage, a perspective, that is quite simply privileged.

No single factor brings this crisis upon us. A concatenation of forces drives us quietly toward the edge now. As doubtless you know, given your own keen intelligence, the subtlest of

'You Can Bet On It,' Says One Who Believes in Doomsday

STAR   By John Sherwood   2/21/77
Washington Star Staff Writer

Theodore A. Wertime does not smile often anymore. He has come to know too much, and he himself sounds a little scared about what he hears coming from his own mouth. Fact is, he is talking to the hills.

He sees the most ominous storm clouds gathering and says the signs are everywhere for everyone to see. Our time is up, he warns. The affluent American way of life as we "knew" it (he uses the past tense) is already over. Our houses are obsolete. Our transportation system is obsolete. The way we live is obsolete, and if we don't act now, we ourselves may become obsolete.

Wertime doesn't fool around with his words. "We don't have time to hedge and haw," he says.

THE BIG PROBLEM is complacency: Through an "incredible quirk in man's society through history," he says, we can assimilate gross changes in a very short time span, yet somehow assume that things remain basically unchanged and enduring. Our own curve of affluence started the plunge to the bottom in 1970, and he believes the point of no return is 1990.

A Smithsonian research associate specializing in man's uses and waste of energy and early pyrotechnology, Wertime is a doomsday prophet. He believes that is what this country faces unless it stops what could be an irreversible downhill slide to disaster.

"To the end," he says, "it was unbelieving that (Rome) could be sacked as it had sacked other countries."

We are currently in the third and greatest of the world's energy crises because of our dependence on fossil fuels, a dependence that began in primitive times. Natural gas supplies will be running out within a few years, and by the early part of the 21st century, oil will be exhausted. "You can bet on it," says Wertime. Coal is plentiful (a 200-year re-

serve), but no one is willing to tear the country apart to get at it.

Wertime, who espouses what he calls "The New Sod-House Frontier," is currently building a solar-heated, ferro-cement house half buried in the side of a Pennsylvania mountain. This guy is really taking his own words seriously.

And he commutes to work in an old VW bug.

He says the OPEC oil nations accept the fate of their oil eventually running out before we will even think about accepting our fate of them being unable to supply it to us. In the meantime, we grow more and more dependent upon them

while they realistically plan to grow less and less dependent upon us.

WERTIME GIVES as a perfect example Reston's new futuristic party-underground school called "Terraset" ("set in the earth"), which opens tomorrow. Its $600,000 solar heating and cooling unit was funded by a grant from the government of Saudi Arabia, the world's largest storehouse of oil. The U.S. Energy Research and Development Administration had turned down the funding request.

Unless we begin tracking down new ways to exploit solar and hydrogen energy sources by 1980 at the latest, we are in most serious trouble, he says.

"This summer, electrical brownouts will be commonplace," he predicts. "There just won't be the power to operate our air-conditioners full-blast anymore. And gas prices will continue to rise (gas is $2.75 a gallon in Greece) until we are forced to buy smaller cars and turn to bicycles and motorbikes and mass transportation like the jitney bus."

Subway systems, he believes, are obsolete because they are too astronomically expensive to build.

The "barbarism" that has led to our decline, is, without question, the automobile that also gave us our unparalleled freedom. "It is a truly deceitful and malevolent villain. . . . It has helped us in a mere 50 or 60 years to exhaust our great treasure of petroleum fossil fuels and to come complacently to live on imports from OPEC states. It most of all is a symbol of the wasteful society now in transition," he says.

In addition, we are "confronting the most intractable depression since economic curves began to be charted toward the year 1030 A.D. Weare in a crisis of convergence. Things are converging on us from all sides."

SO WHAT TO DO? "Start conserving fuel immediately! Insulate the homes by filling up those empty attics, and especially insulate the north side of the home in the winter and the west side in summer. The only windows should be the ones facing south. If snow melts on your roof, that's an indication that you're a

See DOOM, B-2

Washington Star Photographer Gus Leus
Dr. Theodore A. Wertime: The time is now.

crises will always prove the most deadly. You recall how I used to worry over the risks of Soviet buildup and Chinese aggression, and I was entirely justified in harboring those fears, even if we managed to stave off the worst. What we face now, however, is more corrosive and insidious than overt conflict, as horrendous and unthinkable as a nuclear war might be. Our desecration of the planet must be stopped very promptly, or woe be unto us!

I've written Carter, at the White House, to forewarn him of the dangers, much as Einstein did Roosevelt at the dawn of the nuclear era. We'll see whether Carter proves as prescient and responsive as Roosevelt was.

In the meantime, I want to turn my attention to other matters. You know, I'm sure, that John and Steve have projects in hand now—projects, it is hoped, that will feed their own fires as well as further my causes. John has consented very kindly to join me for the latest of my Mideast expeditions. He'll come along as project manager, and act as liaison between me and the team. It's a major undertaking; I've assembled the best people in a wide array of fields—metallurgy, glass, ceramics, crystallography, even geology. Cyril Stanley Smith is planning to join us, as a sort of "grand old man." We'll take the group to places like Tal-i Iblis, down in the southern part of Iran, that they'd otherwise never get to see in a lifetime. It will be an expedition truly operatic in scope!

I mention all this simply to keep you in mind of the larger canvas. I know that you and Marcia intensely value your independence; and I respect you for that. You've carved a niche for yourself in the world of academe that you inhabit with grace. Having funded Steve and Jackie through those rough times of theirs, and having lent John a hand when he and Suzan needed it (Charlie, of course, is a separate matter), I'm doubly grateful to you for being self-supporting and not making encroachments on the family's resources.

But our survival will depend on our pulling together as a family. I realize this may sound faintly melodramatic to you, but believe me, I've pondered all these issues deep and hard. I speak from experience. We pulled through the Depression— our whole family, Grandma Wertime—as uncrippled as we did because we never lost sight of our essential priorities. Given your efforts to start your own family now (I wish you and Marcia luck), it's vital that we keep our lines of communication open. It's all I ask, at present. I know how busy you are.

Gretta's pups are thriving! Bobby Hunter, down the valley, has adopted one of them; we must still find homes for a couple of the others. We'll keep Bert and Leo. They fit well into our enclave.

My love to you both,
Ted

CYRIL

We've hiked down the valley along the Conococheaque Creek, stopped, removed our shoes, and waded over to the far side. From here the road curves up around the flank of the mountain, buried deep in the autumn leaf-fall, its wagon-carved depression still highly visible in the forest. Then it climbs, winding its way along the flank of the mountain until it turns to the south and starts the long trek westward that leads out to Pittsburgh. The Old Forbes Road. In 1758, that tough, outspoken young Virginian, George Washington, a colonel in command of the forces from Virginia, joined General John Forbes to carve this road directly across the Alleghenies. Their objective—they succeeded—was to take Fort Duquesne from the French.

Now saplings populate the middle of the roadway, and lichen-covered rocks have tumbled down the embankment to impede our forward progress. But it's still a real road after two full centuries. As we're hiking along it now, my father, John, and I, under a pristine autumn sky, we can feel the ghostly presence of the British and American troops, the heavy, lumbering wagons that had traveled this shale surface.

John and my father have recently returned from the Middle East. My father is regaling me with stories of their adventures. The Forbes Road serves as our silent, leafy backdrop. "It was poignant, I tell you. You'd agree, wouldn't you, John! We'd already seen a whole host of silver mines—the Zagros and Alborz are just full of them—but this one was special; it contained soft, pure silver that the miners of antiquity had scooped out with horn tools. So anyway, we were gingerly climbing up this narrow mine shaft that was full of big spiders and no wider than this"—with his hands he estimates a width of thirty inches—"when suddenly we bumped into this dried brown package that was wedged up above us.

"Well! We didn't know what it was. So we backed out of the shaft and brought our archaeologist in. It turned out, for the love of Christ, to be a mummified *child*! You see, they'd sent children in to mine in very tight places, which no doubt resulted in many tragic early deaths. But it was the face on this boy that so much impressed us! As brown and wizened as he was, there was infinite sorrow still embedded in his expression. You could tell it was a young boy from the shape of the features—and, of course, other things."

My father pauses, his eyes fixed on the distance. We've reached a wide outlook in a bend on the mountain where a shelf of sandstone opens. To our west, the Cumberland Valley pours farmlands and orchards into the cup of the horizon.

"Lordy be!" my father says, taking in a deep breath. "What a sight!" He squints.

We linger for a minute, taking drinks from our canteens. Then we're on our way again.

I'm first to speak. "A few minutes ago you said something about Cyril. Something about your getting irritated with him."

"Yes!" says my father.

"So," I ask, "what did he *do*?"

"Well, Cyril, you know, is an arrogant man in his own way. He's been up there presiding for so long at MIT now—"

My brother breaks in. "Why, he's renowned in his field! He's a world-class metallurgist."

"No question!" says my father. His eyebrows lift. "The very best, I grant you. Still, he's stubborn and abrasive, and sometimes he simply doesn't listen to reason!"

"So," I ask, "what happened?"

I glance from my brother to my father.

"Oh, he buggered one of our best and most important experiments. I was interested in the way they smelted copper in southern Iran. When we got to Tal-i Iblis, a crucial metal-making center, he began a quarrel with me about how we should proceed.

"We'd rounded up two of the local workmen to instruct us. In antiquity—as now—they'd used a bellows-blown furnace to smelt copper ores, as well as lead and iron ores. You know, there's something quite uterine about the ancient furnaces; they're womblike, almost, giving birth, as they do, to these strange and occult metals . . . So here we are, anyhow, in Tal-i Iblis, one of the last places on earth where they use these old methods, and Cyril gets it into his mind that we've got it all wrong! 'They didn't smelt copper in a furnace,' he tells me. 'They used crucibles.' Crucibles! Oh, well, *hell*! I knew from our previous studies that crucibles were used for *casting* copper, not smelting it! So I tell Cyril this, and he says no, no, no: they smelted the ores in a crucible! I tell him that we're wasting valuable time doing this. But by God, he insists.

"So these two local fellows set a crucible up for us. And Cyril goes to work on it. And boy, does he ever get the fire pumped up hot! With the help of a hand compressor, he gets it all the way

up to 1200 degrees—*higher* than that, even, according to the thermocouple. *And he melts the crucible!* Produces a *single bead* of copper—and melts the blasted crucible! And then gets furious at *me*. Proclaims it's all my fault! Says I haven't let him go about it the right way . . .

"We had a hell of a time of it. And after that, to be honest, I developed a hatred toward him that was so intense and vivid, I really wanted to kill him!"

My mind casts back over our history with Cyril: Cyril Stanley Smith, the renowned metallurgist. One of the presiding intellects at MIT, a tall, distinguished man, he was already in his sixties by the time I met him.

I never liked Cyril very much myself. I can remember his visiting us in Arlington one time when I was in my late teens; he had taken quite a shine to my mother, as it happened, and every time I turned around he had his hands on her. Never very good at handling awkward situations, she was excitable and girlish. *Lecher!* I thought. *Keep your damned hands off my mother!*

My father had given Cyril, without asking us, a highly prized samurai sword made of the finest beaten steel, which he'd bought, I think, in Hong Kong. We boys had been led to believe that the sword eventually would be ours, and suddenly here it was, being given away to Cyril. We had taken the sword out of its scabbard on occasion, in the presence of our friends, and swung it around our heads like pirates; its blade was like a razor, and it had a clean, unblemished shine that made it beautiful and deadly.

So my father's mention of Cyril stirs mixed emotions in me.

"It's true!" he says now, to both of us, his blue eyes glinting. "I gave a lot of thought to it—what you could do out there in the desert . . . There was one particular moment during the worst part of this trip when I genuinely thought that I could do away with Cyril and no one would know it. We were walking along the edge of this gulch, this ravine, in an especially wild part of the Alborz Mountains; it was a very tricky landscape because the soil was loose and sandy—badlands more than desert, like northern Arizona—and I thought to myself, *Hell, I could just push him over . . .*"

"Cyril has been a good friend of yours," my brother says.

I look over at John; despite the fact that he's a mere fourteen months older than I am, he has an air of authority that I've always lacked.

"That's correct," my father says.

"He was instrumental in getting *The Coming of the Age of Steel* published!"

"I wouldn't say 'instrumental' . . ."

"Why, he *was*," John insists. I keep silent, listening. "I recall it very well! He read the book in manuscript and made valuable suggestions—"

"I grant that," my father answers.

"—at a time when you weren't widely known as a scholar. Besides, his metallurgical knowledge has helped you refine some of your most important thinking—his great knowledge, for example, of metal crystallography. It's something you lack! He's shared generously with you, even if he *is* irritating."

"That's true." My father nods and awaits John's point.

Which he gets. "It's rather grudging, all this talk of killing Cyril."

My father's eyes flare. "John, goddammit, in certain ways he would have had it coming to him! He's manipulative, conniving . . . I've bent over backwards to help Cyril in my turn—brought him along on my expeditions; shown him things, things and places, he would never have seen on his own! And when you think about it hard, it's a point that holds true for half the scientific community—that portion of it, anyhow, with pyrotechnical interests. If it hadn't been for me—why, a good part of this field wouldn't even *exist* today! So if I feel a murderous impulse toward Cyril Stanley Smith—by God, *I don't apologize!*"

"Well," John answers, exhaling in impatience. "Let's just change the subject."

"As you wish!" my father growls.

INFERTILE COUPLE

"Hold your question a sec! Please."

The doctor bends over me, absorbed in his inspection. I've begun to say something, but he quickly interrupts me. His head is faintly tilted. His voice has the monotone of someone preoccupied.

Obedient, I go still.

At last he lifts his head. "Sorry about that," he says. "I needed to concentrate. Varicoceles are hard to spot. I didn't want the distraction."

"Sure," I say.

Again I wait.

The doctor's expression undergoes a sudden change—as if, somehow, I've done something unseemly. His eyes drop. He looks away from me. "You can pull up your shorts now."

I blush. My scalp prickles. How typical of doctors! One minute he's involved with my most private parts, as though he were tuning a piano, and the next he's getting fastidious on me. I mean, I can't read his mind!

Buddy, you're the one who's been fooling with my nuts—

I catch my anger, lifting my Jockeys.

"So—" I say.

He doesn't wait. "I don't find any blockage of the seminal vesicles. You *do* have a slight bulge on both of the ducts, but I don't think those really amount to much of anything." His eyes finally meet mine. He's regained his matter-of-factness. "So I don't believe that a varicocele is your problem."

"Where," I ask, "do we go from here?"

"Well, your motility's a problem. And your count's somewhat low. But with the cold packs and all, those are things that you can make some improvements in. Dr. Ringland will call those shots. He's the specialist here. I'm a urologist, after all."

Whacking off is so delicious when it's furtive and guilt-ridden. But having to do it *on command*—that's another matter. So we're at the hospital for the latest of our efforts, and the only place I can find to perform the task (Dr. Ringland has said "Here," shoved an empty lidded cup at me, and told me to appear at a certain room on the next floor up once I have finished) is the men's room situated inside the X-ray unit. It's next to the men's gowning area. A very cramped bathroom, it contains only space for a toilet and a washstand. No urinal or partition. Just a door, a floor, a light switch. The elemental basics.

And here I am now, trying to get the job done quickly—a very awkward thing under these circumstances. Bartleby, moreover, doesn't choose to cooperate—he'd prefer not to—and glares up at me with a melancholy aspect, an intractable schoolboy.

I've guessed that this bathroom might be a decent bet; when I entered the X-ray unit, there'd been no one around. No footfalls appproaching to suggest I'd be disturbed. It's uncomfortable in here, and logistics must be looked to—keeping the plastic cup ready; not contaminating the lid; finding a suitable position on such an odd toilet seat. It's curiously constructed: half rods, half lacquered wood, most surely not designed to provide any comfort . . .

I sit, racked with thought about all the rough procedures we've been through already in an effort to make a baby: the laparoscopy, the culdoscopy, the samples; count, motility, the urologist's prowling, the charts and thermometers that Marcia's had to use . . . *THIS IS NOT GOING TO WORK*, I almost say aloud. I catch myself quickly. No muttering in here! I've got to do my best now to redirect my thinking. Guide my thoughts into more pleasurable and stimulating pathways.

I settle on Sue. Sue's one of my women, my mythical women. (Does any man lack a store of mythical creatures?)

Sue is a blonde: straight, honey-gold hair drops just past her shoulders. She flips her hair forward, exposing her white neck. Her skin is so faultless, even here on her neck, that it's much like touching the inside of her thigh . . .

I'm beginning to get somewhere!

. . . when suddenly there comes (*oh, no!*) a knock on the door, a sharp *rap rap rap!*

Jesus!

Bartleby plunges. Sue starts to flee, like Eurydice to the underworld. I struggle to detain her, in a hurry to get the job done . . .

"I'll be out in a minute!" I call through the wood, and see, beneath the door (there's an inch-and-a-half gap—*Why so much space?* I wonder), the toes of someone's slippers! Christ, it must be some guy already gowned for an X-ray . . .

Meanwhile, I'm pressing to get this job *finished*, plastic cup at the ready—

—and the voice calls to me, "Look, I have to *go*, buddy!" It's an old man; I can tell from the timbre of his voice. And I answer—trying to be, *O Lord yes, cheerful* (or matter-of-fact, anyway) and get this job over with—"Okay! Just one second now! I'm almost finished!"

But I'm *not* almost finished, nothing like it, and working harder . . .

The old man's fist starts pounding on the door now—*BLAM BLAM BLAM!*—and he says, *"What in the hell are you doing in there anyway, buddy?"*

And suddenly somehow, out of desperation, I've finished—plastic lid on the cup, pants and shirt put to rights—and I exit past the old man (he's bald, white fringes of hair around his skull, puzzled look on his face; besides, I'm a good deal taller than he is) and stride down the hall to find the nearest elevator . . .

. . . and get this baby in the warmer . . .

FEBRUARY WEATHER

The news that Marcia is pregnant galvanizes my family. My parents phone, excited. "Sweetheart," my mother says, "what *wonderful* news! It makes me want to cry!" Noises thread through the phone line.

My father's more measured. "Dick. Congratulations. I'm glad it's finally happened. So! What are your plans now?"

"Well, in fact," I begin, "we've started looking for a house." For years we've poured money into other people's pockets; time to start putting it back into our own.

I'm still saying this when he cuts in on me. "Look. You should. *Absolutely!* Go out and find a place! Your mother and I will help you get one. I mean it quite seriously. I'm sure we can pull the funds together somehow . . . You're welcome. I *know* you're grateful!"

They own a house out on Paros they no longer have any use

for—they could handily, he says, convert it into a down payment with a bit of paperwork . . .

Marcia and I go hunting. We squander several weekends looking at overly costly places—colonial homes with pedigrees; spanking-new split-levels with wet bars in the rec room—all as far beyond our means as the shimmering islands of a distant lagoon.

Our realtor sits us down and confronts us with the limits of our financial possibilities.

We ring up my parents. They tell us not to get discouraged. *"You need a house!"* proclaims my father. *"Don't give up. Stay on the market! It's not going to hurt you if the first one is modest."*

But some are *too* modest: an old slice of building wedged between two stores in the Elkins Park area—itself a store at one time, probably; a beat-up bungalow in a rural backwater amid a wild growth of cedars and untamed pines. After several such busts, we tell our agent, Jackie—she's relatively young still, with frosted blond hair and a tendency toward blue jeans—that maybe we had better sit on it for a while. She promises to call if she finds a good prospect.

In less than a week she phones, her voice excited. "I've got the place for you. But we have to act fast. I've got a jump on the market."

The place, as it turns out, is only four blocks away, on a leafy, curving street, Shoemaker Avenue, right here in Jenkintown.

Jackie meets us there. As we're looking the place over, she says in a low, cautious voice, "It'll take work!"

I can see that myself. In the kitchen there's cracked linoleum, old metal cabinets, a stove caked with grime . . . splintered floors in the dining room, almost beyond repair now . . . the same in some of the other rooms . . . and bad walls, *bad!*, painted over many times, full of nicks and painful gouges. Whoever painted here had no clue about painting, or surface preparation either. Sash cords are broken, panes cracked . . .

The place looks bombed.

But I'm not a man who lacks vision.

It's a three-story twin with a steep slate roof and a collapsing back deck with a garage under it. Right away my eye tells me that this was once a graceful place with high Victorian ceilings and oak sills and moldings. The dining-room bay contains three tall windows, windows that let in a pleasing world of light; and while the living room is small, it, too, has high windows. On the second floor we find a narrow bathroom and three bedrooms, all of decent size. A steep pine stairway gives access to two additional bedrooms on the third floor, the first an angled space facing out to the north and east, with a view that soars over all the local rooftops. My heart grabs at this space; I can see myself up here, making this room my study. The other room contains an old-fashioned gaslight from the early days.

Audrey, the owner, a tall woman, is a real talker. She makes eye contact only if there's something to be gained, though how she calculates her sense of advantage totally eludes me. She's recently divorced. Her ex, Dan DePretis, is a post office worker who (it seems) has cruelly left them. Audrey works; her youngest son spends his whole day at child care. There are three other children, either teens or nearly grown. The bottom line is that Dan co-owns the place and will have to be part of any transaction.

By evening we've signed papers and written the first check. Closing approaches. The money arrives in good order from my parents.

Settlement occurs the day before we move. It's an out-and-out disaster. The DePretises have scarcely gotten any of their stuff out by the time we arrive for the walk-through. The kids are in the basement, throwing trash out the window. It's evident they're frantic; they've built a mountain of litter in the small front yard that soon will be ours. Nothing has been cleaned.

Nothing's swept. Nothing's ready. We see no van for them to put their furniture in.

We complain to their attorney—Jackie has convinced us to go to settlement minus a lawyer—but he stiffs us, escrowing a meager chunk of money for a cleanup afterward and assuring us that the DePretises will be out by nightfall. Word reaches us at the settlement table that the kids, while heaving trash out, have ruptured the water line in the basement. The cellar is flooding. The break is unfortunately on the *street* side of the valve, so the water can't be turned off; a plumber will be needed. The lawyer concedes that of course the DePretises must pay—but *we* will have to hire a plumber.

While the plumber, that night, stands ankle-deep in water, splicing pipe into the main, I glance around in a daze. The cellar has been unswept for so many years now that a thick sandy sediment has formed beneath the water. I pause on the stairs overlooking this dark lake, whose bronze surface shivers in the February chill. Then I wander in a numbed state through the rest of house. My mind fixes idly on an inconsequential matter. We've yet to meet our neighbors, whose house next door is dark (they're in California, I've learned, till the weather gets warmer), but their house already haunts me. A wind chime on their front porch stirs the air with strange music. It's music made of ice cut thinly into razors, of souls captured, grieving, in glassy cylinders of metal. The effect is so eerie on an evening like this (I'm here alone with the plumber; Marcia is over at our old place packing) that as I wander through the upper floors surveying all the damage—*It'll take work! It'll take work!*—I find myself throwing nervous glances over my shoulder and huddling down deeper into my thick hooded sweatshirt.

We move on Lincoln's birthday—February 12. The previous evening, snow had been falling. It's changed over to drizzle now, a fine steady rain little more than a mist. Rotten weather. The temperature hovers somewhere in the low 30s.

My parents have offered to come help us move. We've accepted their offer. They arrive with Charlie at eight o'clock in the morning. Before Marcia and I can even catch a first breath, our apartment is a crucible of Wertime commotion. My father is overbearing in his demand to get started. But I can't pick the rental truck up until eight-thirty; we're also awaiting the arrival of two friends who have offered to help us. We start carrying boxes down the two flights of stairs and putting them out on the porch.

My mother has brought lunch—cold cuts, potato salad, her homemade meat loaf. I'm grateful; I suspect that by the time we break, around noon, we'll all be hungry.

My friends come. We pick up the truck.

With everything loaded, we get under way. My father rides with me. I've omitted the precaution of tying things down because the trip's such a brief one. Just four short blocks. I know enough to ease the van through every turn slowly. It's like carrying an aquarium filled to the brim with water.

Shoemaker Avenue undoes my heart this morning. The February drizzle; the thin veneer of dirty gray snow on the ground; yesterday's closing. It's all too much. And here to greet us at the house, the two large mountains of DePretis trash and discards on either side of the walk. They look like pyres built of wood and broken chair legs, too wet for the match.

"Well, here we are," I say grimly.

I glance at my father, dreading his reaction.

As soon as the van stops, he leaps from the cab and makes his way onto the porch. He pivots, head lifted, as if he's tuning into signals coming from outer space, and scans the whole street. He walks back toward me as I'm climbing out of the truck.

"Dick!" he exclaims. It's his first view of the place, and his eyes are shining. "I knew it! I just knew it!" It isn't hard to tell when my father is happy. "The house. The whole street. It's *just* what I thought it would be!"

"Yeah—" I start to say.

But my father isn't interested in what I have to say. His comments are directed more to himself than me. *"It's exactly like Chambersburg!"* His smile is so wide that his lower teeth show. "I'd said to myself, when I first heard about it, 'I'll bet Dick will find a place that looks like Chambersburg.' And, by God, you did! Why, this could be a block away from Joe and Vee's old place! *You couldn't have done better."*

His eyes drop their blazing benediction upon me.

Dumbly, I send my gaze across the short space that separates me from the house. Sure enough, the red brick is of a Chambersburg color, nearly wine-dark in hue, and about the whole place—the slate roof, the big porch, the holly tree in the yard—there's the feel of central Pennsylvania, the small towns that chain along Route 30 toward the east. I've replicated the past, and not even known it.

The Chambersburg connection energizes my father. He is abruptly everywhere—in the truck, unloading bookshelves; hauling boxes to the third floor, deputizing my two friends to carry in this or that: the heavy sofa, the old sideboard. He orders Charlie all over. He clatters loose bundles of curtain rods into corners, swings lamps onto tables, stuffs our clothes bags into closets. And all the time he's talking. *"Dick, you'll want to get down to work on these floors. Do it right away, before you get yourselves settled! And that rear deck needs shoring—especially if you're going to try to use the garage. See if you can't pick up an I-beam somewhere. Or a pole. A pole would do. You'll need to point some bricks on the wall out back. There's a crack out there that needs emergency patching. I'll bring you a couple of redbuds down from the mountains; you can put 'em by your garden."* He adds that he owns a cast-iron stove he'd like to give us. A wood-burning stove. We could install it in the basement for extra heat in the winter . . .

By the time we break for lunch the move is two-thirds fin-ished, and my father is hoping that they can hit the road by three. This doesn't keep him, though, from holding forth for everybody (my friends more than the family) on the latest of his notions about energy conservation, the state of the nation, his Mideast expedition, his most recent finds about ancient smelt-ing in Anatolia. He's as spellbinding as ever, his mind weaving back and forth across North Africa, the Tigris and the Euphrates, Turkey, Iran.

We resume. Groans, some laughter. By the time we've fin-ished, it's just before four and my father is chafing to get on the road. He'll come back, he tells me, within a couple of weeks in order to "do some planning" with us, though he doesn't elabo-rate. The front-porch roof needs some major rebuilding; we can do it, he hopes, over my spring break. I agree to all he says, too tired to protest.

When at last the day is over and our friends have finally left, Marcia and I glumly survey the damage. We're shipwrecked together on some far-distant shore, the evidence of catastrophe strewn all about us.

Our cat, a quiet creature, walks back and forth between us, rubbing against our legs and sizing up her new home.

"Poor Boots," I say. I lean over and pick her up. She's a stray we'd adopted three years ago, a rangy mongrel, steel-black except for her front paws, which are dipped in white ink.

Marcia says, "She's not happy."

I laugh. "It's no wonder." The cat does a flip to escape from my arms and lands neatly on the floor, her last tail joint twitch-ing. She stalks away from us.

Marcia asks how I'm doing. I ask her the same. We develop our plans for the cleanup ahead. I tell her I don't want her to push herself too hard. When she gives me a blank look, I point to her belly. She's just begun to show now; it's her second trimester. "Oh," she says, "that."

"*That*,'" I say, mimicking. "You *are* pregnant, aren't you?"

"Humpf! Much *you'd* know," she says to me, drolly. We laugh with exhaustion.

Ownership is lowering its weight on me already. "Let's go the hell out," I say to her finally. "It's no night to cook."

VIOLENT REVOLUTION

The dream is an old one. The dark corridors of a long, winding basement have led me many floors beneath a gigantic building, a templelike structure that rises above me, tier upon tier; I can look up through this building while I'm still far beneath it because it floats over me like the bottom of a glassy ship glimpsed from the seabed.

Then the dream alters, and I'm being chased over land by a silent locomotive, just the engine, a diesel. My chest fills with fear, and as I flee, I ask myself, *But how can this train proceed without any tracks?* No matter where I hide, the diesel pursues me: up pine-blistered hillsides, over bridges, down pavements, across meadows dotted by scrubby lone cedars . . .

I awake in a sweat. My hand gropes for Marcia, but she's already up. I fall back, groaning. This dream of the diesel always yanks me awake, leaving me amazed that I've been asleep at all. The *silence* of the pursuer is the thing when I've awakened that clings to me most. The terrifying quiet of the chase. The utter silence.

I breathe out. Sunlight splashes on our heavy bedcover. A breeze pushes in through the half-opened window.

I stretch, examining my ten extended fingers. We've taken the front bedroom until the plastering is finished in the room we *really* want, the middle one on the same floor. Like the dining room downstairs, it has large bay windows.

Today my father comes to discuss things with us. His phone calls have alluded to some "paperwork" he'll bring, and there are the repairs on the house he wants to talk over with me.

My mind has been distracted. I've been occupied these weeks (just two since we moved in) with the nightmarish cleaning that everything, *everything*, in this house has required. The grime in the kitchen has been the worst of it.

He arrives around lunchtime. We offer food. He declines, saying he's headed over to Aunt Selma's after he's touched base with us. She lives in West Chester, about an hour from here. But he will, he continues, gladly accept our hospitality when he comes back to help me rebuild the porch roof. That'll be in three weeks.

He has brought a set of papers my mother has typed up, which he asks us to sign. They're IOU's, of all things, stipulating that should he and my mother, at any point, want back the down payment that they have given us for this house, we will put the house on the market and refund the money to them. One of the documents names them as co-owners of our place.

There's more, an agreement they want Marcia to sign; it would make over to them a certain portion of her inheritance. Since she's due, my father says, "to come into substantial assets," it strikes them as fair that they be pledged a share of them. As "collateral on their investment." Just how much is unclear, but it ought to be substantial.

Marcia and I are confounded. We are flat-out amazed. But my father is oblivious. "You see, it's just a kind of quid pro quo," he explains. "If it's all down in writing, there'll be no confusion."

"But Ted," Marcia answers, when our stunned silence has ended, "I have no idea what my inheritance is going to be! My grandmother *and* my parents will have to die first. Anyway, I doubt if I'm legally entitled to sign any of it over—to you and Peg, or *anybody*."

My father's eyebrows lift. "Well," he says. His eyes go steely.

I find my voice, finally. "Dad, it's a lot to think about." My expression is beseeching. "We really need some time to think all of this over. We'll act in good faith."

"Right you are," says my father. He rotates his shoulders slightly and slackens his lower jaw. I sense that he's mollified, at least for the moment.

He abruptly switches subjects. "Have you found an I-beam yet?" I'm about to say no when he jumps in again. "You should find one soon. You don't want that whole back deck collapsing on you. A pole will do, as I said. A good strong steel pole."

I say I'm on the lookout.

"Good," he says. "Work at it."

"Ted," says Marcia, "can't we offer you at least a cup of tea or something?"

"No," he says, turning to me. "I have to go soon."

We discuss the repairs we'll undertake on the front-porch roof. He'll bring his truck and a ladder—and the woodstove as well, weather permitting. He urges me to solicit one of my friends to give us a hand: we could use a third strong back for a couple of hours.

As he's heading for the door, he says, "Oh, incidentally. When I return in three weeks, I want you to save a bit of time for me. I'd like you to glance at several of my recent manuscripts. I'd value your comments."

"I'd be glad to," I tell him. "By all means, bring them!" I'm perplexed by his tone, which seems to imply that I might begrudge him this.

"Good," he says. He sets his jaw. "Well—till then!"

And he's gone. In a cloud of IOU's.

The very first morning of my spring break, he returns as proposed to help me fix the porch roof. At least the weather cheers me. The last several weeks have been blustery, often raw despite intervals of sunshine, and punctuated by unpleasant discussions about my parents' "documents." I've tried to convince Marcia, who is very angry about them, that, as nutty as they are, they're a gesture more than anything. We won't have to sign them, won't be held to them, ever. She's not so sure.

But today is a real gift—cloudless and windless, the temperature well up in the 70s already. It may get as high as 80.

Marcia and I have shopped for food we know my father likes: steaks for dinner; special cold cuts; lots of juices, fresh and bottled; pumpernickel bread. Eggs and bacon for breakfast.

We'll have good appetites, I'm sure of that much. My father loves to be out in the sunshine, and I have fond memories of our roofing the two houses at the mountain place together when I was seventeen or so.

He has brought the woodstove; pristine cast iron, it sits in the back of his yellow Dodge pickup, a number of its fixtures still wrapped in gray cardboard. He's also brought his ladder, a big power saw, and a handful of other tools.

Right away my father asks, "Do you have that friend coming?"

I regret to tell him no. "All my friends are away. It's their spring break, too."

"Well. You can rustle up a neighbor to help with the stove."

"That shouldn't be a problem."

My father is dressed in a ball cap, khaki pants, a dirty white T-shirt, and a pair of frayed sneakers. I notice how broad his back looks in the T-shirt, how strong his arms are. He's well tanned already, although it's only mid-March.

We can get onto the porch roof by climbing the ladder, or we can step out onto it through our bedroom window, whose sill, oddly enough, is just a foot above the roof. It's a big enough roof—some thirty feet long and almost fifteen feet wide—so our work is cut out for us. Within minutes we discover that several of the main beams have totally rotted. We'll have to replace these, redeck this section, and then put down the new roofing.

By 11 a.m. we've bought all the supplies and are up in the sun stripping off the old surface. It clatters—a sooty rain, shards of shingles mixed with nails—into the broad gravel drive we share with our neighbors, who are still in California.

Getting the supplies has been an uncomfortable experience. We've taken my father's truck to two home-supply outlets, where he has exerted pressure on me to spend some serious money. I haven't anticipated getting new gutters and downspouts, as well as hangers to go with them, in addition to the roofing paper, nails, beams, and plywood. He's prevailed upon me, finally, on the grounds that we ought to go ahead and get the whole job done. When, back home, Marcia learns what the bill has been, more than double our expectations, she gets upset. The day seems to be off to an unlucky start.

Still, by lunchtime at one o'clock we've finished all the beam work and have decked the large bald spot we've created in the process. With the help of a neighbor, we've wrestled the wood-stove off the truck into the basement. We've also managed to get the whole roof stripped.

After lunch our pace quickens. My father is infused with a fresh bolt of energy and goes into high gear, setting his jaw, the perspiration gleaming on the back of his neck. It's time to haul rolls of felt up onto the roof so we can get started nailing. Having carried up two rolls, my father says, "Fetch another. We need one more." I scamper down the ladder and throw a roll on my shoulder. But when I step on the bottom rung and start to lift myself up, my leg starts to tremble and my knee goes slack. My father, seeing this, descends the ladder without speaking, throws the same roll on his shoulder, and climbs back up without effort.

I clamber up behind him. Marcia has appeared in the window to our bedroom, her stomach on a level with the white windowsill. She's just begun to wear maternity dresses; there's something slightly plaintive about her posture as she stands there. She's wearing a green jumper, and her long brown hair puts her face in a mournful frame. "Can you help me?" she asks.

"Sure."

I climb through the window, telling my father over my shoulder that I'll be right back. I remove my leather work gloves. The room is so dim after all the bright sunlight that I'm momentarily off balance. "What is it?" I ask her.

"Oh, it's this take-home exam!" she says. She's begun her graduate studies full-time at this point, hoping to finish her basic coursework before the baby comes.

She wants my help, she says, in organizing her answer to the big essay question. She explains the problem to me and shows me the pages she's written in her small, rounded hand.

"Well, look," I tell her. "Remember what I said to you about this this morning—that you're trying to pack too much in all at once? Here." I point. "You can open this whole section out."

"But if I do that *here*," she says in agitation, "I won't have anything left to say in the *final* section!"

"*Sure* you will!" I say. "You can . . ." I pause, scanning her writing briefly. "Remind me again—the name of this course."

"Successful Strategies for Community Planning."

I ponder for a moment. She breaks my silence, her eyes misted over. "Damn it, I *hate* this! I can't seem to get—"

My father calls me: "*Dick!*"

I put my head out the window, saying I'll be right there. I pull my head in and continue. "So anyway. *Here* I'd—"

Marcia breaks in again. "Oh, I wish that you didn't have to do all this roofing! I really need your help with this!"

"Well, look," I say, "I've got to go. But try"—my tone's encouraging—"to expand your introductory section. It'll work better that way."

She looks at me forlornly as I climb through the window.

When I'm back out on the roof, my father glares at me. "Dick, we have to keep moving!"

"I understand that."

I look over at him. He's on his hands and knees, face shadowed by his ball cap, pounding a fistful of flathead nails in.

I'm begrimed with dirt and sweat and light-headed from the sun when Marcia calls again, perhaps forty minutes later. Again she's in the window. This time I say, without ceremony, "What?"

"I need to talk with you."

I climb through the window and exhale hotly.

"Don't be angry," she pleads.

"We've got a *lot* to do," I say. I look at her severely, noticing how much taller I am than she is. It's a trick of the sunlight. I feel slightly dizzy; I could really use a hat. "Okay. What's the problem?"

I expect it to be her exam, but she says, "It's Boots. There's something wrong with her. I think it's really serious."

My brain explodes. "The *cat?*"

"Yes. The cat! Come look. She falls over when she walks."

"Marsh. *Look*," I say. My shoes are rooted to the carpet. "I don't have time to deal with *Boots* right now. We're—"

Marcia glares at me. "Well, we can't just ignore her! I think she's really sick. I had *told* you she wasn't doing well when we moved in here."

"You said she wasn't *happy*. Don't you remember? She'd flipped out of my arms and landed perfectly on the floor. That's not *ill*."

"*Dick!*" my father hollers.

"I think," Marcia says, "we ought to take her to the vet."

Again my father calls.

I turn back to my wife. "I can't deal with this right now, Marsh! It'll just have to wait." She starts to protest, but I cut her off: "*Please*."

And climb back on the roof.

My father is irked. I can feel his vibrations. "Dick. *Look*," he says. "This is a big job we're doing. I really think that we have to keep at it now." I agree, but he persists. "These breaks you're taking for Marcia are just slowing us down."

Under my breath I mutter, "Well, now it's the damn *cat*."

"Whatever!" he says, and bends back to the work.

The sunlight washes over me. *Why do these two*, I say to myself, *these two people whom I love perhaps more than anyone else in the world, need to be putting me under this kind of pressure? Why must they fight for my attention like this?*

We break from our work at five. My father gets the first shower; by the time I've finished mine and put on fresh clothes, he has settled on the sofa, his manuscripts around him. He's relaxed into loafers, dark-blue trousers, and an ivory dress shirt. You would think from looking at him that he's spent the whole day on his scholarly pursuits. My own face is sunburned.

My father, it seems, has gotten past his irritation. He's ready now to draw me into the precincts of his thinking. Legs crossed, hair combed, he sits awaiting my attention.

I give it to him freely. Marcia comes and goes, rejoining us now and then.

This is all right with my father; it's my focus, really, that he wants fixed on him. "Well!" he says, once I've settled. I've pulled the front curtains open to keep the room a little cooler—it's a hot evening still, surprisingly so for the season—and a pleasant bluish light has spread itself through the living room. I sit facing him in the old green wing chair. "I want to share with you some of my recent ideas about a number of things," he says. "The world, you know, right now—"

I interrupt. "But first," I say, "tell me about your manuscripts! Give me a broader sense of where your work is heading right now."

He says he'd be happy to. He has become engrossed, he tells me, in the latest scholarly discussion about "interfaces" between varied aspects of the ancient material world. "Glass. Ceramics. *Cement*. The full range of metals. Iron. Copper. Tin. Bronze. The fire-based technologies as well as those that aren't fired-based. Wood, for example. We're beginning to understand—Hans Wolf, for instance, saw this out in Iran, in things like the construction of ancient waterwheels—that wood was a much more crucial material, even in early desert cultures, than we'd realized before. It was crucial to the pyrotechnical industries, too, since it fueled the vast need for charcoal in iron reduction, not to mention ceramic kilns and the slaking of limestone . . . The need for wood was almost endless. So! These are among the topics that these new papers cover. I've also, as you well know"—Marcia now has joined us; my father unfolds and refolds his legs, as if to acknowledge that his audience has widened—"conducted this protracted scholarly feud with Colin Renfrew over the whole great so-called dispersionist controversy. Renfrew, you remember—"

"Ted," says Marcia softly, "can you explain that to *me*?"

While my father is detailing the bare bones of it—the question of whether culture is dispersed from single centers or innovations occur at the same time in different parts of the world—I'm thinking, *Interfaces*. No question that it's one of the more popular new words, but to my ear it's jargon, like *societal* or like *impact* employed as a verb. To hear it used so casually rubs the ends of my nerves.

Yes. Well. *Interfaces*.

By the time I've reconnected to the drift of his discourse, my father has changed direction. He's onto a new theme. ". . . So I'm counting, you see," he says, speaking not to me but to Marcia, "on Dick to be my ally . . ."

I ask him to back up, apologizing for my lapse here.

"Why, I was just telling Marcia, though it's no news to you: I see dire things coming! The world that we're living in is a very dangerous place." His eyebrows arch. "Very, very dangerous. Dangerous, indeed, beyond our wildest surmises. You remember those pieces I'd published in the *Post*? I'd written you about this. They stopped running my articles because my message unnerved them. And that's right! It *should* have! Those folks at the *Post* thought I was going off half-cocked when, in reality, I was setting down the *plain truth* of things! And the White House turned out to be even worse than the *Post*. James Fallows wrote me a *one-line response*—and a very condescending one—in answer to the warnings I'd sent to President Carter! In our energy consumption we are facing a crisis now of *unimaginable proportions*—one that will threaten the stability of the West and put the Middle Eastern countries—the Arabs especially, with their vast oil reserves—in the global driver's seat. Already they're buying up huge sections of London and the other capitals of Europe—for *cash*, for the love of God! *For cold cash! Oil* cash! And meanwhile our leaders are going down the primrose path into an energy dependency on other nations so drastic that our quality of life here could plummet! *In an instant!*"

My father pauses here to let his words sink in. His furnace is white-hot now. "So. I'm preparing for the advent of a new revolution. Yes!" he says. His eyes widen. "It may startle you to hear

it. But it's a stark fact: it'll happen. It grieves me, in fact. But we'll have to be ready for it. It was one of the reasons that I built that house of mine on the top of a mountain, in a place as apparently out-of-the-way as McConnellsburg—it affords a certain kind of . . . security, let's say. I've even had a second well drilled within the last month so we'll have plenty of water. And we're stockpiling goods against the time when we'll need them. So." He halts. "I need allies. I'm frankly not sure that John and Steve will be among them, though I hope that they will be. They're uncommitted at this point. I fear they just can't see the future all that clearly. But I'm counting on Dick."

I inhale slowly and say to my father, "These are interesting pronouncements." I pause for a second. "What do you have in mind, exactly?"

"I'm not sure," he says. "It'll depend a great deal, frankly, on just *how* things develop. So: I want you two to have your home base here, of course. But you *also* need to know that we'll have room for you—you and the others in the family—in the McConnellsburg house. If and when you might need it. And you may very well! Bobby Hunter has already shown his willingness to stand with me. So have several of my neighbors. The world may get *quite* dangerous—much sooner than we realize!"

When my father has finished, I look at him soberly. The room curls about me, a tunnel linking us in the dim tides of evening. I realize that Marcia has slipped away at some point and made her way upstairs. I can hear her on the second floor, making faint noises.

I exhale in caution, hoping that I don't disturb the air between us too much.

"Well," I say to him slowly, "I've certainly always trusted your judgments of things. Very interesting! All of it. What you've had to say just now."

He looks at me. "Yes. Well!" His eyebrow lift. "Enough," he says, "of my preachments."

Marcia has come halfway down the stairs. Leaning forward, she asks me to come up to our bedroom for a minute.

Smiling, I rise. I turn to my father. "We'll talk more of this."

I climb the stairs to my wife.

At the top, she steers me down the hall to our bedroom. I'm just about to ask her if she has heard what he's been saying when she shuts the bedroom door and says flatly, "*Look* at her."

I turn my head, puzzled. It takes me a second to respond to her directive.

"*Look!*" she repeats.

Boots has become a low black stain on the carpet making odd jagged motions. I need a couple of instants to decipher her movements and several more seconds to transform what I see into full comprehension. Our adopted cat is struggling, attempting to walk. With every step she takes, one paw or another—a front paw, a back one—crumples beneath her and she keels over sideways. She's struggling, fighting. Up she goes once more, gaining a moment's balance, lurching; then she keels over again.

The sight goes into me like a hot piece of metal.

"Jesus," I murmur. I cross the rug to her. She lifts her head toward me, her white whiskers spread. Her mouth starts to open, but before a sound can escape her, she has fallen once again.

Marcia is crying. "You see what I mean? This isn't just your dumb neurotic wife butting in. Your pregnant wife who interrupts your big conversations! This poor cat needs *help*!"

I stand there at a loss, Boots a weight in my arms.

"But Marsh—"

She interrupts me. "You can't be so preoccupied with yourself! There are other concerns here!"

"Look . . ." I say to her.

But she will not relieve me. Her eyes bear down on me, burning brown coals. "We are simply going to have to take this cat to the vet!"

"Yeah, but when?"

"*Now*," she says.

"*Now?* We haven't eaten dinner!"

"It'll have to wait," she says.

This idea so stuns me that I finally gather courage. "Marsh! Why can't this wait? I mean, if we have to go tonight, we could eat first, *then* take her—and hell, for that matter, you could take her by *yourself* . . ."

"I can't believe you'd say that."

"Well, look, honey. Jesus! We've been working all day! My father's come down here and put out all this effort—"

"Don't shout at me."

"Hey. Listen. I'm not shouting." I speak sotto voce, though it takes an effort. "And we've been planning this weekend for quite a long time now—"

"It's not," she says, "the only thing that has to be done this weekend."

"Hey. Come on. That's not fair. I've helped with your exam."

"Yes," she says, "you have. Some."

My chest contracts. "The reason I said you could maybe take her by yourself is that—"

"Dick!" she breaks in. "I can't drive the car and hold the cat in my lap! I'm *pregnant*, for God's sake!"

"But why does Boots need to be held?"

"She's sick! Can't you *see*? I just can't throw the poor cat in the car." Marcia's eyes are bright with tears now.

"I still can't see why—if we have to do this—it can't be after dinner."

"I've already called the vet," she says. "They're open till six-thirty. It's Saturday, remember?"

My head's in a vise. "Christ. All right," I say, and fetch a deep breath.

The news that we're running off does not please my father. He takes it like a stoic, his head tilted slightly. He stares directly at me. I offer him a blizzard of explanations and apologies, and hasty reassurances that the dinner will be a good one once we're back.

His manuscripts? Surely. I'll have time for them—am looking forward to them . . .

"All right," he says. His voice has gone flat. He adds that he'll go up and take a nap while we're gone.

Marcia drives while I hold the cat in my lap. The evening unfolds as I gaze through the windshield, its sunshine slanting on the west sides of the houses. I scarcely see the streets and neighborhoods we pass through.

The trip takes twenty minutes. In the vet's waiting room I feel nothing but numbness. We're the only ones present.

We wait.

We wait longer.

I let my eye go prowling. It's a typical vet's waiting area: fake wood paneling; linoleum that reeks of dog and cat urine and a pine disinfectant; the acrid smell of animals in the kennels. A fish tank forms a partition of sorts between the receptionist's desk and the chairs we sit in. I hand the cat to Marcia, lifting its claws from my pants legs, and walk over for a look. The tank holds a dozen fish: three large angelfish that drift in frozen postures and a bunch of smaller tigers that dart up and down. The aerator dispenses its column of bubbles in the tank's far corner. A ceramic ship's anchor and a miniature castle, also of ceramic, are the tank's sole decorations, although a pair of green plants wave their fronds like sea anemones.

I gaze at this tank while my father's strange pronouncements swirl through my mind. I think to myself, spontaneously, *This Alamut shit . . .*

The connection suddenly hits me. Jesus. Precisely! A newly dug well; the stockpiling of things. His citadel, all of us huddled into it . . .

I'm thrown back years, into the mountains of Iran.

The vet is a short, dark-haired woman in a lab coat, with a foreign-sounding accent. She invites us to set the cat on a clean stainless-steel table. We describe the problem to her. She examines Boots abstractedly, in a meditative silence, asking few questions. "It's a shame," she says finally, "that they can't say what's hurting them, the way people can. It's one of the challenges of being a vet."

But she's certain enough, she says, of the nature of the problem: a degenerative breakdown of the central nervous system. They could do some exploratory tests, she explains, but they'd be quite invasive. Operations, in fact. She turns over a white paw. We might spare Boots that. "How old is this cat now?"

"We don't know," we tell her. "She's a stray. We simply found her."

"Well," she says, looking at us, "it's hard to say how long now. Make her comfortable, if you can."

When we return, my father is up from his nap. He's back on the sofa looking through his manuscripts.

He nods at us briefly. Marcia takes pains to explain the situation, her voice as cordial to him as she knows how to make it. But he chooses not to listen. As soon as she goes into the kitchen to work on dinner, he turns and says to me, "I'd like you to get started reading now. If you don't mind."

I say, "Of course!" But something to drink first. "Can I get you anything?"

He says, "Thanks, no. Well, some juice, I guess. Juice."

I return with glasses filled with two different juices and offer them to him; he opts for the cider. I take the lemonade and start in on his manuscripts. There must be eighty, ninety pages all told.

I dig in, determined to make good on my promise. The first piece discusses the range of critical temperatures in ancient smelting furnaces in Jordan, Turkey, and Iran. For a while all goes well. But I reach a point suddenly when my mind starts to glaze and I falter over terms that I know perfectly well: *molybdenum, manganese*. My hand goes to my forehead. The truth just hits me: between the day's labors and the long hours of sunlight, I'm failing. I'm exhausted.

Dinner revives me. We eat in relative quiet, making desultory chat about the members of the family. My father talks briefly about his latest publications, and this seems to refresh him; renewed by *his* refreshment, I make a few comments about the manuscripts I've looked at—stylistic comments, mainly; also points on organization—and am left feeling consoled that we've moved beyond the worst of it, this interruption for the cat. At meal's end, Marcia is content to give my father and me some private time together. She withdraws upstairs while he and I are still busy eating our ice cream.

So it comes as a jolt when my father says, without prologue, "Dick, if you were younger, I'd give you a whipping." My spoon halts in midair, a clump of vanilla dropping off onto the table. "I couldn't be any more furious with you! It makes me feel savage."

I plunge through a trapdoor. All the icy looks that I've had from my father over the course of a lifetime have been nothing next to this. His eyes sear into me, blue drills, heated.

My bowels turn watery. I try to speak, but my jaw shakes.

"I'm of a good mind," he says, "to go ahead and clear out!"

"No, don't," I say. "Please."

"Well, I am! I really am, after what I've been through here!"

"Look," I say, pleading. I'm trembling so hard now that my words take a rough, guttural tumble from my throat. "You'd lose if you did that. You'd lose a lot more than you'd gain, if you left now."

These words are meant to placate. But my father mistakes them—construes them instead as an insolent threat. His eyes widen, glaring, and the ice that I had felt driving at me seconds earlier becomes an arctic blast. He bares his lower teeth; his strong jaw is clenched. He scrapes his chair back half a foot from the table, and I can feel the hair rising at the base of my neck.

I brace myself. I can't help it.

For the longest of moments we stare at each other. I don't dare to speak. When this moment has finally passed, I say to him, the words a bone lodged in my throat, "Look, I'll make it up to you."

At this, he lifts his shoulders and sends his gaze across the room. I watch him intently, studying his profile—the stubborn, perfect chin; the still-handsome features.

"All right, then," he says, as though he's made a concession at a very heavy price. "But I'll probably head out on you fairly early tomorrow. I have my own work to do."

"No quarrel. You've been a great help today."

"And now," he says, "if you'll read."

He rises from the table.

"I'll be interested in your comments first thing tomorrow."

I watch him as he heads toward the bottom of the stairs. There's the slightest hint of a stoop to his thick, massive shoulders. It's the curve of an object filled with force, like a coiled spring.

The manuscripts confound me. The pages multiply in a crazed, random fashion; the paper grows sharp-edged and heavy as I fumble. I seem lost in a building filled with pits and strange mirrors, and before I've been immersed in the task for even an hour, I feel the way I do when I'm driving late at night: the slightest tilt of the wheel sends the roadway tipping over. *The destruction of ancient forests . . . the presence of lead oxide as a . . . local clays molded into . . .*

I halt. My thumbs plunge into the depths of my eye sockets to reignite vision. I stretch my mouth wide and unroll my facial muscles. Nothing is working. I get up, go to the kitchen, slice myself a hard apple. Wedge of cheese on the side. Marcia comes in to announce she's going to bed; I spare her the encounter I've had with my father. I'll be up for a while, I say. She says that she'll keep Boots in with us tonight. I nod as she leaves.

I return to my struggles. I'm determined to complete all of my father's manuscripts, though an inner voice is saying, *Why the hell bother? How can he profit from your reading these pages? What do YOU know about these arcane matters?* The answers, of course, are clear to me—they're engraved on the hard, flat fact that "reason" is not the point here, or "need" either. But I pose the questions anyway. I cling to the notion that there's more at issue here than just bizarre subjugation, although there *is* that, too; that my judgments do, somehow, matter to my father, even if I can't understand exactly why; that, strangely, without them he'd spin in a darkness whose dimensions I can only guess at. *This unfathomable man—*

And suddenly I've broken through the wall of my exhaustion (the apple? the cheddar?) and escaped into that hard, brutal late-night clarity that steely persistence sometimes affords us. My mind clears, condenses, pools down into itself to a point of white focus where all distractions melt away, and I'm left with a pure, clear nugget of concentration. "I'll pay for this!" I think, knowing perfectly well that payment will take the form of a dull gray bar, one stretching out through the night into morning: an alertness that will fix itself in wakeful abstraction until just before dawn, when I'll tip into sleep for a fitful half hour.

I will pay for this. I'll pay.

But I will finish his manuscripts.

When I come downstairs the next morning, my father has already eaten. I am brushed by the memory of how often, during vacations, he'd rouse us from sleep to get started on some project (on, of course, *his* schedule, always) and how the cracked, dry taste of an unfulfilled night would linger in my mouth until I'd had some breakfast.

I glance at him warily.

"Eggs and bacon? I'd be happy."

"Thanks, no," he says. "I've had a bowl of shredded wheat."

"You're sure?"

"The cereal's fine. You could pour me some juice." He pauses. "Let me hear now how you've assessed my scholarship."

I would have liked to eat first, but a glance from him persuades me to eat and talk at the same time. I carry his manuscripts to the table with a bowl of sliced peaches and a tall glass of milk. I sit for some seconds, staring at his pages. *Christ. Exactly what . . . ?* A desolating panic locks onto my throat. The typed words are like tadpoles, inky squiggles swimming in a vague white liquid.

But the sun tumbles in through the dining-room windows, my vision suddenly clears, and it all comes back to me. "Okay!" I say, ready. "I really liked some of these, especially the way . . ."

Not all my comments are positive, however. My father takes my words as he might an injection—good for his health, if not altogether pleasant. He glances, as I'm talking, slightly down and to the side, the way deaf people do to make the best use of their hearing.

It's a half hour later by the time we've concluded, and Marcia has entered.

"Well, Dick," says my father, "I appreciate the effort. I value your comments. You've a good eye for my foibles, and you have an uncanny way of understanding good *structure.*"

I return the compliment; I'm really impressed by the way his writing has strengthened in the past half decade. As a stylist, especially, he's gained a fluency and ease that are really impressive.

These are genuine compliments; I think my father knows it, if only from the bluntness implicit in my praise: *Whereas earlier in your writing . . .*

We are finished with his scholarship. Before I even know it, we're up on the porch roof again, our work clothes on. A scattering of squirrels are making noises in the treetops.

Again the day is splendid. Dry, bright sky, no wind. It's early enough still that shadows from our neighbor's house make pockets of dimness on the flank of our house; in these pockets the air still holds a pleasing chill. It'll be hot soon enough.

I can see through the window that Boots lies immobile in her basket near our bed. The sight of her grips me. My father and I work quickly, hammers lifting and falling, the graveled rolls of roofing paper unspooling now. *They'll have to forgive us,* I'm thinking about our neighbors, whose Sunday peace we've shattered. *The whole place will look better for the work that we're doing. The house. The neighborhood.*

My father soon insists that we start hanging gutters. He'll leave it to me, he says, to finish up the roof. I nod, saying nothing, and we haul up from the driveway the white aluminum gutters and pristine new downspouts. Up come the hangers, and we get started nailing.

It's during one of our pauses that the second of the weekend's major crises erupts. I've dropped into the kitchen and filled glasses with cider, which I've carried out to the porch, where my father awaits me. As I'm handing him his cider, he bares his teeth at me from under his ball cap. He says—again no prologue—"Dick, I'll tell you something." He glances past my shoulder. I know where he's looking: through the beveled glass pane in our oak front door to where Marcia is sitting. She's at the dining-room table touching up her exam, which she intends to drop off today, even though it's Sunday.

He looks at me hard. "I've been caught in a power play here this weekend, as you saw last night. It's foolish, what you've done. Your mother and I have given our support to your efforts, have shown you *great* patience; we've gone to some lengths to make it feasible for you to have a place of your own. And we've had *small thanks,* frankly."

On this note he pauses. I stand there mutely, my tongue wrapped in shackles, my coward's heart neither affirming nor denying.

"And there's something else I'll tell you. You know well enough now about some of my more basic dissatisfactions"— here his jaw juts forward—"my dissatisfactions with your mother.

With Charlie. I won't hesitate, I can tell you—*I won't hesitate!*—to go off at this point and start myself a new family. I'll do it! In a *minute!*" He shuffles toward me with small, mincing steps. "And I'm absolutely serious about the shape of things to come. There's a revolution needed to set this country to rights that may involve the tragic smashing of all the old vessels. I'm not looking for the leadership role in whatever unfolds now, but if fate thrusts the role upon me, by God, I'll *take* it! So I can't have my position compromised at this point. You recall my saying, last night, that I have the support of some of the people who live on the mountain, certain people down in the valley. Well. I found myself faced with an ugly situation lately. Gretta and her pups, I learned, had taken to roaming onto other people's property, knocking over their trash cans and getting into their garbage. I just couldn't have it. I just couldn't afford to lose my base of support—have it threatened or eroded by a dog, a mere dog. So. You know what I did?"

Just the slightest pause here.

"I took Gretta out and shot her. *Yes*, by God! I shot her! I gave her a couple of swift kicks and put a bullet in her brain. With that old gun of yours. And I'll tell you, it *grieved* me. I'm a peace-loving man, and I abhor such violence! But I had no choice! There is simply *no way* that I can see things jeopardized, let them *be* jeopardized, at this critical juncture! It upset your mother, of course, but there was *just no other way*! I can't be worried if it displeases people. The time must be served!"

The empty juice glasses ride my grip into the house like a pair of scorched chalices being borne to a sanctuary. At the table, Marcia halts me. "What has *happened*?" she asks me. "You're as white as a sheet!"

I set the glasses down. I feel my Adam's apple bob.

"He's shot Gretta," I tell her.

"*What?*"

"He's shot Gretta. In the head. With my old rifle."

Before the words are out, even, Marcia has stood and wrapped her arms around my chest, her head on my shoulder. I feel her tears on my neck. "Oh, honey. Oh, God. Oh, that poor dog," she's saying.

But my eyes have glazed over, and her words seem to reach me from the bottom of a well. Their echoes rise toward me like the tendrils of a plant struggling up toward the sunlight. I'm barely able to hear them.

For in my mind I'm on the porch still, listening to my father. He has landed himself on the river's far shore, oaring over in a craft whose pitch-covered hull is black with the weight of an irreversible action. Later I will ask myself, *Do I see the fear in him? As I stand here watching, as I stand here listening, is his fear visible to me?*

By the time I've turned and walked indoors with the empty glasses, I'm a thousand years older.

Things blur on me. There's an odd matter-of-factness to the immediate sequel: Marcia and I end our conversation quickly, our voices lowered to a murmur; I rejoin my father on the crown of the porch roof, where we take up our labors, hammers whanging and rebounding. Our exertions throw a curtain up around the words he's spoken, a heavy velvet curtain that renders everything theatrical, unreal, histrionic. Marcia makes an exit for her drive across town. So it's just the two of us. We work for about an hour.

He decides it's time to go.

I offer him a sandwich. He accepts; he'll take it with him. While I'm busy in the kitchen, the refrigerator's cool air offering its balm, he clatters his equipment into the rear of his truck.

By the time I go back out, he's been upstairs already to gather his things. He's ready to depart now. I hand the bag to him. "I've put some juice in here to go with your sandwich. There's fruit, too. And chips."

"I'm leaving the ladder here," he says. "I'm sure you'll need it." I thank him, protesting, but he says, "I have another. Just don't leave it sitting out in the rain. Give it a coat of varnish at least once a year."

I'll take care of it, I promise him.

"Now, look," he says to me, his eyes going hard again. "It's crucial that you and I understand each other. We've helped you get started. It's entirely up to you now. If you and Marcia flounder, I will not rescue you. *I will not rescue you!*" For a third time this weekend, he bares his teeth at me. "It'll rest on your shoulders. Don't come to me if you find yourselves sinking!"

I nod. "I understand." I offer conciliatory words, but he's already gone; his pickup has vanished through the trees at the corner, its throaty sound lingering for the briefest of seconds.

I scan the street. It's vacant. Wearily I turn and make my way back up the ladder. Time suspends itself while the afternoon passes, and I stubbornly finish the rest of the roof. By four o'clock I'm so stiff that my knees and ankles ache, and I change to a sitting position in order to continue nailing. The seat of my pants is getting grittier.

Marcia returns at the moment I'm finishing. I call to her from the porch roof and climb down the ladder.

"Exam in?" I ask. I extract a handkerchief from my damp rear pocket and sponge my begrimed face.

"You and I have to talk," she says.

She draws me indoors. Decisively she sets her leather folder on the table.

"What?" I say.

"Your father. I stopped by my parents' after dropping off my paper and told them about Gretta. They were very upset."

"And well they might be!"

"Dick," declares Marcia, "your father is *disturbed*."

"You're telling *me* something?"

"I don't think we can trust him. I—"

"Hey, wait a second. Do you think I'm *blind*?"

"No, but—"

"Marsh, goddammit, you don't know the half of it!" Heatedly I tell her about the parting shot he'd taken—the business about his leaving us to flounder on our own—and then relate in more detail what had happened on the porch: his threat to march off and start himself a new family, the "revolution" stuff—oh yes, that again!—and all the crazy talk about his "allies" on the mountain. "So," I finish, out of breath, "don't for a minute—please!—suppose that I don't get it. I mean, son of a bitch!"

I've dropped into a chair at the dining-room table. Marcia, behind me, sets her hand on my shoulder, intending to reassure me. After the weekend we've just had, her touch irritates me. *Goddammit, woman!* I think to myself. *Just look at the harm done! If only you hadn't had to meddle so much . . .*

But I check the wild impulse. We're beyond that now.

I tell her I'm going out to take a short walk. I climb the stairs, not looking back. Drop myself in a hot shower for a brief three minutes. Dress. Go downstairs. Step outside.

The afternoon's light seems to be forced down my throat, so tightened do I feel in my father's aftermath. A train in the distance wedges its rumble into my hearing, and I find myself thinking how grotesque it is to be living in a world as relatively civilized as this—and yet to feel endangered, as I do, by my own father. *By my own father!* The more I think about it, the more I feel the hackles rise on the back of my neck. Steel bands tighten across the width of my chest.

I turn toward home. When I get there, I tell Marcia, "I'm going to call my mother."

"What good will that do?"

"Shed light, maybe. I don't know."

"You think so?"

"It's worth a try, I guess."

"Well, I'll tell you *this* much," Marcia says, drawing herself up. "I've made up my mind while you were out walking. If your father shows up at this house unannounced, we're going *right* out the back door! We'll run. Or call for help. Because we're not going to wait around *here* for him to shoot us. I know too much about men who turn their guns against the members of their families."

This jolts me afresh. Yet I see, in a second, how close this stands to my own fearful thinking.

I dial the phone and get my mother. Our talk is a bizarre one. *"Oh, Dick, it was terrible, what he did to that dog; I tried to stop him . . . Revolution? My word! REALLY? No . . . he's made no mention of it, not that I can recall . . . Yes, I agree, it's disturbing. Well, he's under a lot of stress . . . SHOOT people?! No!"* Laughter. *"Oh, I wouldn't worry, sweetheart; if he shoots somebody, I'm sure it won't be anybody in the family!"*

I hang up, stunned. I say to Marcia, "I can't believe it." I relate the phone call to her. She's as nonplussed as I am. I call my brother John and have the same conversation. *"If he shoots somebody, Dick, I'm sure it won't be any one of us!"*

"They don't *get* it!" I tell Marcia. "They don't fucking *get* it! Are *we* cuckoo here?"

"Not for a minute," she says flatly. "Dick, your family's crazy. Your *father* is, at any rate. We have to protect ourselves against him. Ourselves *and* our baby."

I am coming unglued. Time to laugh and cry together, hoot and dance, dig for cover. I feel like a puppet whose strings have been snipped. I have just made my way through the two longest days in the history of the planet. And yesterday was—what? March 15.

The Ides of March.

It could have been you, Cyril! I find myself thinking. *You were just damn lucky.*

Almost two years will pass before I see my father again. By that time, he'll be dying of cancer.

CATALINA

Twenty-four years old, he is a private in the Army. On a certain date at midnight, having set aside his uniform and donned civilian clothing, he enters a woodland clearing north of Los Angeles. There he confers with high-ranking members of the American military about the strategic bombings of Germany that he has helped to plan.

He has finished his basic training at Fort Meade, in Maryland, and a train has carried him to California. He has been told to wear his uniform during his trek across the country, but he carries special orders instructing him to change into civilian clothing once he's reached his destination.

At the age of twenty-three, he had been hired by the Board of Economic Warfare, whose mission is to cripple the industrial and economic structures of enemy powers. He has been elevated to one of its innermost circles, the Joint Target Group. Already he is an expert on the bombing of German cities. The government had wanted to send him to England to join the war effort there, but his hometown draft board, in southern Pennsylvania, had other plans for him. He is not unhappy. He aims to help win this war, is a fighter by nature, and wants to keep the rank of private so that there is no distinction between him and other men. Why should his education or intellectual achievements make any difference?

The Joint Target Group has not been prepared to let him go. Although he has been drafted, he has continued to meet with its members at their headquarters in D.C. — even during the weeks he is in basic training. It has been determined, moreover, that his talents will be needed in the OSS. He has been sent to a secret school to undergo special training as a hand-to-hand killer and demolitions expert, and he has been schooled in jungle warfare. Some of the OSS brass had wanted to send him to Officer Candidate School, but others thought that he was too valuable to be spared for the months he would need to attend OCS.

He has another mission before traveling back East. He must spend a week on the island of Catalina, in the windswept reserve on the wild, uninhabited northwestern part of the island that faces away from the California mainland. It is the last of his tests as an expert in survival and basic jungle warfare. He has a knife, nothing more. He will live by his wits and eat off the land. At the end of the week, he will be ferried to the mainland to take the train east before being sent to India, the stopover that awaits him on his way to southern China.

He is dropped off on Catalina. An Army cutter carries him out there in the dead of the night and deposits him at a certain point on the northern windward shore, a rugged part of the island. He wears combat fatigues and carries a well-honed dagger. Standard issue, steel-handled. He enjoys the feel of it; its handle fits smoothly into his well-callused palm, and the blade has the width, *almost, of a bowie knife. He has learned tricks with it and can keep it razor-sharp on the leather of his high-tops.*

What he knows about Catalina would fill a very small book. He has been briefed at training camp about his pickup point at the end of the week—a small cove tucked into the western side of the island—and afforded some details about the island's plants and wildlife. He has supplemented this by stealing away for an hour to the Library of Congress while he's been in Washington to help plan further bombings. He has speed-read a pamphlet about Catalina compiled in the late 1930s by the editor of the island's newspaper. He's aware that it is an oddly severed island: there is Wrigley's island paradise on the southeast, where the hotels and spas thrive; then there is this rugged section, the giant military reserve, windswept and austere. He has found the island's archaeological treasures of interest, and also the history of its mining—two of the scientific interests that will dominate his life. He has memorized the map.

He finds himself now in the section called the Isthmus, whose shape is intriguing to him. It replicates perfectly that of a Woodland arrowhead, down to the fluting. The coast consists of a series of concave bends and coves, backed by hills that in places drop sharply to the water.

It's a clear, starry night, the wind off the Pacific coming steadily and coolly; he will reconnoiter this section of the island in the morning. His best chance for sleeping is on a high, flat rock, since there are scorpions and rattlers. He cuts oleander to use as a blanket and smiles to think that he'll be sleeping under poison. His best bet for food lies in the wild goats on the island. He has heard that their flesh, which he'll eat uncooked, tastes very much like monkey . . .

He is on a plane over China, on his way to Kunming, when the first of the atomic bombs falls on Japan.

FIVE

THE PICNIC IN THE RIVER

It's happening to me. I am coming unglued. I can't keep things in steady focus with my eyes; my fingertips are numb; a steady wind blows at me, and yet ruffles nothing. My feet seem to hover several inches off the ground.

At first I attribute it to nerves and exhaustion. The stress of work, overwork; the courses I'm teaching; the extra jobs I've taken on to meet the bills coming in; my jumping up at all hours to feed or change our son, David, who is just months old now; my efforts—frantic ones—to keep up with this house, which drinks repairs and money as a thirsty man does water. I almost feel that my father's parting words have become a malediction: *"If you start to flounder, I will not rescue you!"*

By October I know better. This is *not* just exhaustion. There is something wrong with me.

It started with a leaf, a simple leaf. On a tree branch. I was staring at a maple leaf turning red outside our window and blinked at it suddenly. It disappeared on me. Not exactly disappeared; but winked like a light, like a carnival light, say, or a shiny piece of foil rotating in the sun. Soon I'd discovered that the whole world glittered. Nothing was stable. My eyes wouldn't focus.

Now other symptoms are occurring: a feeling that my feet are off the ground, a floating sensation; a silent, nonexistent wind that seems to blow through me; a numbness that spreads up and down both arms, deadening my fingers. My hearing has dulled. I will suddenly grow dizzy right after drinking something, something ordinary—milk, water—and I feel bloodless at times, my legs and feet heavy. Perhaps worst of all, the world has receded: I've been cut off from it by panes of thick glass. This glass wraps around me, encases me, airless. I live in a cylinder.

What is wrong with me?

I can neither concentrate—concentrate very clearly—nor discard stubborn notions. I'll be standing in the kitchen preparing dinner or washing dishes and suddenly, unexpectedly, not know where I am. A spoon in my hand? Why this spoon? Or a dishtowel? . . .

Odd things obsess me. I cannot, for example, get my mind off a memory of our time in Iran that echoes in my skull like a gunshot in a canyon: the picnic in the river.

The picnic in the river! . . . We've reached Isfahan during a long journey south to Persepolis and Shiraz. It's a dust-blinding journey over the rough washboard roads. Smashed gravel in the desert. Mountains by the hour; merciless sun beating down on us; a cruel baked landscape brought down from the moon. We're making this trip in my parents' big sedan bearing diplomatic plates; piloting it is Tighva, my father's private driver, an Iranian Hassid, in his early seventies now, who has seen persecution, been robbed, lost his business. He's emotional, inept behind the wheel of a car, but bright, good-hearted. And the soul of patience with us: John, Steve, Charlie, my father, and finally me. Yet another of our all-male excursions.

I don't know it now, but I'm descending into illness. Tainted food, it could be. The day after this, the fever will arrive at our hotel to claim me, accompanied by its caravan of death-threatening symptoms. In the meantime, a lightness of head makes the sky bright, unbearably brilliant; my temples are pounding. So our experience in the river unfolds before me in a blister of sensations, bright, kaleidoscopic.

Isfahan. A bridge. An ancient bridge of red stone. No, not ancient; medieval. Merely medieval! Built, Tighva tells us in his accented English, by Allah Verdi Kahn. *Who is Allah Verdi Khan? . . .* But it makes no difference; we are crossing his bridge now, our heavy car crunching on the bones of this dead man. His trolls cannot stop us. It's a fine arched bridge that spans a shallow, sandy river. And what do we see here? I *must* be going crazy, though I don't know I'm ill yet. For down below us in the water, in the smooth stretches separated by the undulant grasses, lie Persian carpets by the dozens, as orderly as soldiers. Laid out like free dollars on the top of a table.

My chest muscles tighten, and laughter stabs the back of my throat. *Rugs in the water!* Hilarity overtakes me. Tighva has slowed our big black Ford to a snail's pace; we're the only bridge traffic in the hot noon hour. It's over a hundred degrees. We peer into the water. Rugs! Ruby. Emerald. Sapphire. Turquoise. Yellow. Hues of a rainbow. *"You see, they fix the dyes here, vegetable dyes. The cold water . . ."* Tighva is speaking, but I hear very little. I can't help laughing. Maybe I'm shouting.

At the end of the bridge we swing off the roadway. Suddenly we're lurching down the tan clay embankment and . . . *driving into the water!* Charlie starts screaming; I grip the seat ahead, unnerved by the motion, no longer laughing. My father is shouting, *"It's all right! It's all right! Tighva knows what he's doing!"* I look out the window. We're a boat now, not an auto.

"It's shallow here," says Tighva. *"You do not have to fear, boys!"*

Slowly, slowly, slowly, the car pulls its way into the center of the river on the smooth, sandy bottom, avoiding the carpets, which we gape at, astonished. Drowned carpets staring with calm eyes at the sun . . .

Tighva pilots us alongside an abutment on the shady side of the bridge; we park in the river and climb out, our feet bare, the steady current tugging at us.

We're going to have a picnic! Right here! In the river! Tighva has prepared it. We'll spread out our blankets on the platform of the abutment . . . A *picnic in the river!* . . .

The heat, perhaps, has gotten to me more than I know, or else it's my illness. When we wade to the car after we're all finished eating, I'm surprised to catch my image in its curved black surface, in the bend of the fender just below the back window. It's a convex surface that distorts my face forward, enlarging my nose to enormous proportions and pushing my ears farther back on my head. It drags my mouth downward so that I look like a mole.

But it's my eyes that most jolt me. We've picnicked in the shade, and I've become unmindful that I'm wearing sunglasses, glasses whose lenses are impenetrably dark. These, in the reflection, become gigantic insect eyes—hideous and bulging, surreal-looking, like grasshopper eyes under a magnifying glass. For an eerie split second that makes my gut recoil, I don't know whether I possess two or eight eyes, or a hundred and eighty.

Jesus, the thought hits me. *You've just seen yourself! Is this what you look like?*

I fight against this notion as nausea rises in me. But the poison has taken. By eight o'clock that evening, my illness is mounting. For the next two days I scarcely know where I am. I sway back and forth in a hammock made of fever, assaulted by dreams: dreams of huge bug eyes, of faces enlarging in a strange hall of mirrors.

. . .

I need help. I know it. I will, in fact, seek it—but not soon enough. Not fast enough to keep the locked valves from opening or the high mountain snows from melting and cascading. It all pours out: my feelings of remissness toward my mother and father, toward Marcia, *everybody*! . . . Guilt over old sins, long dead and buried . . . A sense that my successes (I've just been granted both tenure and a promotion and been made chairman of my department; *The Hudson Review* has published some of my fiction) are ill-gotten, somehow—eloquent testimonies to my rottenness at the core . . .

Sorrow pours over me, a hurricane smashing everything.

I find myself back in the precincts of a therapist. Life has blurred on me. Plain things elude me. I can't grasp, for instance, why Marcia has been so infused with rage lately.

"*My God*," she screams, "*you've become so dangerous!*"

(How am I so dangerous? I don't understand.)

"*You spook me!*" she says. "*You're so goddamn hostile! Can't you see what you're DOING?*"

(Nor do I understand the logic of its being *my* job, and mine so exclusively, to care for the baby and tend to the house.)

"*You're so resentful about everything!*"

"But Marsh—"

"*I have SCHOOL! You want me to work? Well, then, Buster, I have to FINISH!*"

"But Marsh—"

Then it rotates and *I* become the enraged one. She's bossy, a withholder, a lousy housekeeper, a reluctant parent, even . . .

We slog our way through months as my own long-pent-up feelings turn me into a volcano. I'm introduced, for the first time, to the pleasures of being imperious: I quarrel in an instant, subjugate when I can, restrain myself from violence by the merest of hairsbreadths, enjoy vituperating.

. . .

A year after the blowup with my father, I'm bitter toward Marcia as well as him, bitter about the tug-of-war they'd both caught me in over the roof and the cat—

No. It won't do. It's no good for David, this war that we're having. No good for any of us.

I brake the great machine of my bitterness and anger. I begin, very gradually, to gain some control. We're *not* joined at the hip; my issues are my issues, Marcia's are hers . . .

Some dozen months later, we have struggled toward détente. By then my mother has called with the news.

My father has been sent to the Hershey Medical Center. They've opened him up. The cancer has spread so much already that they can't operate.

In a wink, I'm decisive: We're driving to McConnellsburg.

Marcia says, "I still don't trust him."

"So live with it!" I tell her.

But she *is* sympathetic. She will not resist our going.

A weight is lifted from me. I know well enough from my relationships with other people—Grandma Wertime in particular, who'd died years ago—that there's no second chance.

We will head west to see him.

RE-GREETING

He scarcely looks ill! It's the first thought that strikes me when I see him in the doorway; yes, his face has thinned, and the patches of gray at his temples have broadened, but his shoulders are still square, his bearing light.

He seems himself.

A warmth moves into me, a mellow, trusting feeling: there's a rightness to all this. And my father is smiling, a smile that stretches wide to reveal his one gold filling . . .

Our son, David, is with us, in Marcia's arms right now. For the very first time, he's here to see his grandfather.

Still, it makes me feel strange to be up here again, on my father's mountaintop, after all that has happened. Alterations, maybe growth — David's birth; the months of bitterness on my part, on Marcia's . . .

We've been through a lot.

But above all, here's David, his hair as soft and puffy as dandelion fluff. His smile melts everyone. His eyes lock on my father as my father makes his way toward us. I see why, suddenly: my father has a young kitten perched on his shoulder, a striped orange tabby who is shifting like a surfer as my father approaches. The kitten's whiskers twitch as if to help him keep his balance, and his ears turn like radar. Before my father has reached us, the cat has made a circuit around the back of his neck and come down his other shoulder.

David takes a lunge toward this man and his kitten as soon as the two of them reach us. No shyness on David's part! He transfers easily into my father's waiting arms, squealing for the kitten—something like "*Kee*-ee!"—as he shifts his weight over.

"Please come in!" my father says.

Gladness lights his face, David locked on his hip. The cat's in David's arms now.

My brother John is here with his young son and wife. Suzan, an Iranian, is years younger than John; they'd met in Tehran while John was working on a Princeton Ph.D. in Near East studies, one he never quite finished. He's become a rug merchant, a scholar of carpets. Their son, Sam (pronounced, in the Persian fashion, *Sahm*), is a merry three-year-old with his mother's bright dark eyes and olive-hued skin.

John is a tower. At six feet two-and-a-half inches—Thomas Jefferson's height—he stands nearly half a head taller than I do. He's an imposing Nordic figure: white hair, sandy beard, a complexion that does not favor the sun. His preferring to speak Persian with his wife has made him something of a mystery to me. It's a rough-sounding tongue, one I know little of, all cutting gutturals and glottals pitched deep in the cavern of the throat.

Still, it pleases me to see them, even if the news that has brought us together forms a grim set of tidings.

Pancreatic cancer.

I'd first heard about it on the phone some weeks back, when my mother had urged us to come out to see them. She'd assured us herself that Joan would not be here this time. And indeed she isn't, though she's still in the picture. She's in D.C. this weekend.

My father wears a cardigan over an open-collar shirt, polished loafers, gray slacks. I can see now that his ankles have grown visibly thinner and that his wrists are more fragile. It's hard to believe he's only sixty. I can't avoid the memory of how easily he'd waltzed up the ladder that March weekend, those heavy rolls of roofing paper tossed on his shoulder . . .

His chemotherapy treatments are about to begin. "God only knows what they'll do to me!" he's saying. "Make my hair fall out, probably. And leave me feeling like hell. But they're my best shot at this point."

He's trying to sound casual, but I can hear it in his voice: the uncertainty. The tension.

He had returned from the latest of his Mideast expeditions for the Smithsonian Institution feeling rotten and losing weight. At first he'd thought it was his old dysentery flaring up on him. "I'd contracted a nasty case in the Burmese jungle back in the early 1950s, when I'd worked for the State Department. But there was something else, too: everything I ate started tasting like shit."

My mother cuts in. "I knew something was wrong with your father just as soon as he got back! His skin looked so gray . . . He just wasn't himself!"

My father glares at her as if she's committed an infraction. But he says, "Your mother's right. I had no pep at all. I was dragging myself around. So. Then the rounds of visits to the doctors began." Urologists. Internists. *Several* internists. A couple of GPs who had been recommended. "I'd learn, later on, that each of these doctors was handing on to the next one the same set of files."

"What did the files say?" I ask.

"That I was neurotic!" says my father, raising his brows. "*Neurotic*, for Christ's sake! 'Ted, you don't need me. You need a psychiatrist,' they'd tell me."

A polite tinsel of laughter. Even my father smiles at this.

"So I finally started saying, 'Christ, I know *that* already! That I'm neurotic isn't news. But *it's not the problem!*'"

There's a stillness, a pause, at this delicate juncture. We're reluctant so much as to shift in our chairs.

"So I finally got put onto this young Navy doctor. Right here, in Chambersburg. First he gave me just a routine exam. But he was thorough. Incredibly thorough! Then he took me into his office and sat me down in a chair. 'Ted,' he said to me, 'I want you to describe what's going on in you. Whatever is on your mind. We're in no hurry here.'

"I talked for an hour! I told him about every last one of my symptoms! The diarrhea. The taste of food. My energy loss. All of it. And did he ever listen! By God, he was focused. He was like a man listening to—I don't know what.

"At the end of that hour, he put it straight to me. 'I want you,' he said, 'to go to Harrisburg. Tomorrow. We're going to go do a CAT scan on you.'" My father takes a deep breath, uncharacteristic of him. "And there it was. Already spreading. He arranged for a surgeon to operate the next day. But it was too late already; too late for the knife."

A cathedral silence follows, one that lasts only briefly. Sam and David have sensed that the grown-ups' story has ended. They renew their commotion. My father lifts David back up on his lap, nuzzling his flyaway hair with his chin—his fourth and youngest grandson. Sam whirls in circles while he sings a Persian ditty. It makes everybody laugh.

My lips have gone dry. I feel no wish to gloat here. I hear no talk of violent revolution, or of herding the whole family in beneath this mountain rooftop. My eyes take a journey to the barrel-vaulted ceiling, to its rough cement texture and the spots

along its curve where the harem lamps—the filigreed lamps that hang on long copper chains—drop. Water stains, from leaks, have formed small streaks on the ceiling.

We break for food my mother has fixed—the whole tribe of us, that is, except my father. It's clear he'll eat nothing.

Then we resume the conversation. I say to my father, "You must be angry with those doctors."

My brother answers for him, a tremor to his voice. "They were very irresponsible. Dad and Mom ought to sue them."

"We've written letters," says my mother.

"Letters?"

"To the doctors." My mother's face tightens. "They were just jackasses! They didn't pay any real attention to your father. Here—you and Marcia can see what they wrote back to us. John. Would you get the letters?"

John unfolds himself slowly. He returns within seconds.

My mother hands around several sheets of folded paper. When they make their way to me, I glance at them quickly.

"As you can see," my mother says, "they're very careful with their words."

"Yeah, I see that," I murmur. The phrase *occult cancer* occurs in a number of them. "It sounds as if they're duplicating one another, almost."

"Well, that's the problem," says my father, "with this pancreatic cancer. It *is* occult. By the time it's detected, it's too late already."

My mother is roused to a fresh fighting spirit. "But Ted," she protests, "*that* doesn't exonerate—" She halts, turning to me: "Is that the right word, Dick, 'exonerate'?" When I don't answer, she goes on. "That doesn't exonerate any of these doctors. They ought to have been more careful."

My father grows Buddha-like. His shoulders settle slightly. He looks around at all of us, his blue eyes clear. At John. At me. Marcia. Suzan. Everybody.

He turns to my mother. "Peg," he says calmly, "I don't question that." He looks straight at her. "But I am where I am."

The rest of his attention is reserved for his grandsons. As we've been talking, the two boys have been squirming around on his lap, their backs pushed firmly into the comfort of his stomach. One of them jumps up, reaching for the kitten, while the other nestles in. The kitten hovers nearby, just out of reach.

My father leans forward and gathers in both boys. Gruffly he nuzzles the neck of each with his whiskers. They squeal, protesting, tickled, and nestle into him more tightly.

PICASSO

I'm glad to have seen him. I'm pleased he's met David and done so well by him. But the simple truth is that he is who he is, I am who I am. It's hard to know for certain how much can be mended now. In the months that follow, I seem to behold him across a growing distance, as if we're two men standing on separating ice shelves, helpless in the face of the oceanic currents.

The next of our get-togethers drives the point home.

Hot early summer. The thermometer hiked up into the 90s, humidity brimming. A cousin of mine, one of Aunt Selma's daughters, is marrying. My younger cousin Jean.

The wedding takes place in the Devon horse country west of Philadelphia, at a handsome old farm turned into a conference center. A rustic red barn has been refitted as a dining hall.

Swimming pool. Lush gardens. The blooming rhododendrons make vivid splashes. The air is fragrant, heavy.

We arrive a bit late. The service is being held on the big flagstone patio adjacent to the pool; the rows of folding chairs are already almost filled, so we sit near the back. Jean's father, Uncle Jim, is a music professor. Four string players in black tuxedos have already struck up a pleasant piece of Mozart. I don't envy them; I've already melted through my own suit jacket and wish we had been offered some protection from the sun.

My eye scans the crowd as I look for my family. David starts fussing; he squirms in his good clothes and whines about swimming in the pool. We'd been told that there'd be swimming and encouraged to bring our suits. We've brought only David's. We hush him, promising he'll swim after the service.

The wedding march starts. Still no sight of my family. They're all supposed to be here: Steve and his wife, Jackie; John and Suzan; my brothers' two youngsters; Charlie; my parents. I find myself distracted by a frail elderly gentleman who sits toward the front. His hat takes my eye. It's a stiff-brimmed straw hat, very wide; wide enough, in fact, to prevent me from seeing the people right in front of him, who may be my family. Irritation grips me, a sense of vexation with this wizened old fellow. A cane rides his lap; his large, leathery ears protrude from the sides of his narrow white head.

Then it hits me.

It's my father.

This sudden glimpse of him sets a whirlpool going in me. I'm relieved to have found him, even though I'm numbed by his appearance; and yet, at the same time, I'm moved by my old familiar mixture of emotions. My forearms go bloodless, and a tightness attaches to the base of my throat. Things have happened since our last visit with him: yet another family crisis.

It's Joan, Joan and my mother. All the plots, it seems, have thickened.

My father has insisted on a final expedition to his favorite Mideast countries. But the only participants have been him and Joan. They've been gone for six weeks, visiting old mines and caves and various museums despite my father's failing health. Their return has resulted in bizarre, violent fights—fights so bitter that my mother has had to part them and, at times, protect Joan, whose drinking has increased as my father has declined. My father has phoned Joan's parents, who live out West, and urged the two of them to have their daughter committed. According to my mother, even Joan herself has said that maybe institutionalization would be best for her.

This in itself is enough to make my head spin. It's just the tip of it. My father, in a reprise of the IOU business, has badgered my mother to consent to have Joan live with her once he has died—and wants her to sign an agreement to that effect! A cohabitation agreement. My mother has checked with Uncle Rudy on this (he's a seasoned old lawyer) and learned that such an agreement would be legally binding. It would, in effect, grant Joan half-ownership of the house and the property.

Beyond this, my father has grown insistent with my mother that she leave on the weekends—so that he and Joan, he says, can have their "privacy" together. Strangely enough, my mother has acceded, driving down to Fairlington to stay with Grandma Schultz, whose health, too, is failing, or else going into Chambersburg to stay with Joe and Vee. Charlie, in the meantime, has been sharing a sparsely furnished apartment with a young reporter who works in McConnellsburg.

Rudy has come to my mother's defense, offering to negotiate a divorce for her. So far she's declined on two separate grounds—"I love your father!" she has told me, but she's also said, "Well, where would I be if I divorced your father, Dick? I could be left penniless. And after all these years, I don't intend to be!" (A rather different matter from love, as I see it.)

My father, on his part, has grown even more combative. In the hospital again for a fresh round of tests, he has continued to fight. From his hospital bed he has sent my mother a letter on Smithsonian stationery, written, as usual, in his rapid, scrawling hand. She has sent me a copy.

2:00 a.m.
June 29, 1981

Dearest Peg—

Since we had no opportunity to be together to talk privately in the hospital, I write you this brief note.

With the impending end of Joan's sabbatical and a return to a city and a job she hates—and with little money and no apartment—her nights have literally become nightmares and her days moments of cowering in fear in her rooms at the Materials Lab. She is literally at the end of her tether and contemplating death.

Quite frankly, the effort by some family members to put her in cold storage has had its effect and has added to her feeling of isolation. If it drives her to further desperation I shall personally hold the family accountable. I am now approaching a new breakpoint in the treatment of this cancer where I may have to turn to radiation, and where Joan's intervention may be decisive in keeping me alive. I intend for this and other reasons to help her get re-established in Washington and searching for a new job.

There are irrationalities in the situation, but if one were to explore my side of the situation, he would see they are not all on my side.

I must be quite blunt in saying that if the family wants me around and facing the awful facts of chemotherapy—with 3 bad weeks out of 4—then the psychological warfare must stop at once, and that goes for everyone, from Charlie to P.J. to Vee to Clara. Without me, there *is* no family.

Your position in my love is fixed, but I am also a desperate person at a breakpoint *WITH A STRONGLY DECLINING SENSE OF RESPONSIBILITY TO FAMILY, ONE AND*

ALL—ESPECIALLY IF ANY FURTHER DISSENSION OCCURS.

So welcome me home and let us have the pleasantest of times.

All my love,
Ted

I've read this letter in a state of amazement, sobered by its threats and confounded by the grandeur of the claims inherent in it (*"Without me, there is no family"*). It's odd that my father hasn't numbered *me* among his several antagonists, since I've recently put my oar in—felt that I *had* to. When I'd heard about the papers that would enfranchise Joan, the ones he'd tried to force my mother to sign, I finally lost patience and confronted him about it. Our phone conversation became an open shouting match. *"None of YOU helped me build my house!"* my father screamed. *"Well, Kent did, some. Joan was at my side every step of the effort! She's been my companion for six years now!"*

"But Dad!" I shouted back. *"You're not talking a lousy six years with us! You're talking a total of forty years, for the love of Pete. FORTY YEARS of family history! What the devil's going on?"*

He couldn't really answer, and in fact hung up on me. Still, I must have reached him; he desisted shortly thereafter. My mother signed nothing. The subject never came up between him and me again.

Jean's wedding ceremony concluded, we thread our way forward through the crowd to my family. My father has risen by the time we get to him, his cane gripped tightly, his shoulder blades jutting through his seersucker suit jacket. He's wearing dark glasses.

"We saved seats for you!" he says with some emphasis. No further greeting from behind his dark lenses. "When you failed to show up, we had to let others take them."

"We were late," I say simply. We say hello to the rest of the family.

My father's face is parched. His skin is thin and red, pulled taut over his cheekbones. His lips are desiccated; whenever he smiles, his teeth show yellow. His weight has plummeted.

David starts whining that he wants to take a swim. I feel caught. We really ought to make our way through the receiving line. My mother intervenes, volunteering to take him. I protest. She insists; Uncle Jim and Aunt Selma will understand, she says. Soon she and David are walking off hand in hand. Minutes later we see him splashing in the pool with a group of other children.

When the big meal is over and the guests are dispersing, Marcia and I invite my family to come back to our house. It's a spur-of-the-moment offer. My family accepts. We'll lead them over; their cars will follow. David is the only one reluctant to depart. Under my mother's watchful eye, he'd been in the water for an hour and could have easily spent the whole day in the pool.

It's late afternoon, about five o'clock, when we reach Jenkintown. The sun has gone golden. We throw the house open, all the doors and windows. Mercifully, the place has stayed fairly cool, but there's a breeze we want to catch now. I herd the family through the kitchen onto the rear deck while we get food and drinks.

I turn to my father. Over two years have passed since he last set foot here. I hold the door for him as he steps across the threshold, and I'm almost tempted to take him by the elbow. I want him to feel welcome. I'm mindful of everything: our big March blowup; the tense, more recent altercation over Joan. But there's still my old wish to make peace with him. So I turn to him, smiling, and offer him a comment I've been saving for hours. "I like your hat!" I say. "It makes you look like Picasso."

Which it very much does. He resembles the artist in his advanced years, his bald head covered by his stiff-brimmed hat, his weathered chest bared outside his villa near Antibes, that calculating, predatory look on his face that forever let you know that he was sizing things up, on the alert for the main chance.

My father's eyes flare. He bares his teeth at me and pulls his shoulders back. "*I AM Picasso!*" he declares. "*I AM Picasso!*" His rage growing stronger, he walks on past me. He doesn't look back.

Over sodas and snacks, we learn something more about my father's condition. His terrible appearance—about which he's perfectly candid—is more the consequence of his recent chemotherapy than it is of his cancer, at least for the moment; the tumor itself has significantly diminished, and the doctors have declared him somewhat in remission.

"'Somewhat,'" I repeat. "That's a hell of a prognosis."

"It is!" agrees my father. "But it's the best they can manage. I had those tests, you recall . . . My task *now*—" He pauses; David has begun to climb into his lap. I fear it'll strain him, but he welcomes our son, smiling. "My task," he continues, "is to work to get my strength back. I'm carrying this cane now just as a precaution. In fact, I'm getting ready to cut timber on our place! I've just bought a new saw, and I'll start stacking cords on the north side of the ridge." He turns his head, smiling. "Charlie will help me. Won't you, Charlie?"

"Yeah, okay," says Charlie. It's an answer that leaves my brother staring into space.

Not until later, when bedtime has come and I'm lying in the dark, gazing up at the ceiling, do my feelings finally hit me. *You arrogant son of a bitch!* I think. *Jesus. What pretensions! You are not so much as one-TENTH of Picasso!*

At the same time, I know that the gesture had impressed me. Those words were ones he'd uttered with such a pure, fierce conviction! The claim, in an odd way, had almost been validated by the sheer vehemence of it. *"I AM Picasso!"*

Not once, but twice.

VALENTINE'S DAY

"Yeah. Okay!" I tell my father, and hang up the phone.

What sad news. I repeat it to Marcia as I reach for my coat. She hugs me. We're silent. There isn't much to say, really.

I'd last seen Grandma Schultz the day after Christmas, just seven weeks ago; my father, Charlie, and Marcia had come with me. My mother had visited her earlier that morning. After her first stroke, a mild one, she'd walked with a limp and repeated herself more often, but she could still live alone. The second stroke was tougher; it blurred part of her speech and lamed one leg badly. Even then she stayed mobile. The third and worst stroke sent my grandmother to the nursing home.

I enjoyed our last visit. The facility was a good one—spacious, open hallways; clean, bright rooms. The staff was friendly.

There were flowers on Grandma's table, to which we added our own red roses. Still, my heart sank initially; Grandma's room seemed spartan with its hospital bed, night table, and chair. But the bed had a nice quilt; the windows were hung with drapes, not just thin curtains; the chair was a wing chair, comfortable, well upholstered.

Carol, Grandma's attendant—a Chambersburg woman, I could tell from her accent—had just done Grandma's hair, neatly waved and tinted brown, not the usual awful purple. There were pink bows tied in it. It was clear that Carol cared. We thanked her for her efforts before she withdrew.

My grandmother impressed me. She was sitting in her chair, neatly dressed for the occasion. She was wearing her glasses, and her false teeth were in. Although her eyes had the watery, shifting look of a senile person, she reached into herself and pulled herself up to greet us. It took her a few seconds and some evident hesitation, but she called Marcia Marcia and knew I was Dick. She did her best to tell a joke; it came out garbled, but I admired her for the effort.

As the visit was ending, she struggled to pull herself up into full lucidity. She thanked us for coming and kissed Charlie, Marcia, and me. Her face was wet. She held my hand for an extra second. She said a warm good-bye to my father.

We left her in her wing chair, attended by Carol. As we walked down the hall away from her room, I glanced over my shoulder. It was just a reflex; I expected to see nothing.

What a pleasant surprise it was, then, to see my grandmother in her doorway! When her eyes met mine, she gave a hearty wave that spread a smile across her face and lifted her body up on tiptoe. It was the wave of a younger woman—graceful, energetic, joyful.

I waved back to her, gladness spreading through me. When my other grandmother, Grandma Wertime, was dying, a number of years before this, I was the only one of her twenty-four grandchildren who had gone to see her in the weeks before she died. That death, too, had fallen in winter; February, in fact. *You only get a single chance*, I said to myself.

I break the news to my mother shortly after she's gotten off the bus. It's Valentine's Day. She's made the trip, ironically, to get a weekend away from my father's worsening illness and his constant fights with Joan. A gentle death, as things go: Grandma had just had a bowl of vanilla ice cream. Her head had slumped forward. She was gone in an instant.

I've taken my mother to a restaurant for a cup of hot coffee. She holds my hand across the Formica table, her tears and smiles alternating. It's a poignant moment for me. Her grip is very firm, reminding me that the women in my family have strong hands. Grandma's grip, too, was firm. "You know, Dick," says my mother, "I saw Grandma yesterday. I was at the nursing home. And do you know what she said?" A pause here as my mother dabs tears with a tissue. "She said to me, 'Peggy, I believe I'll die today.' And I said, 'Mother, that's silly! You won't die today!' And she said—she was very calm—'No, I think I'll die today. The Good Lord is going to call me.' I guess she had a sense of it."

I nod. "Not far off!"

My mother's jaw trembles. She reaches for my hand again. "Sweetheart, you couldn't have broken the news any more gently."

We leave for Chambersburg at seven the next morning. We'll pay our respects to my grandmother briefly. She's willed her body to science, as my father has. Her final journey will be to the Hershey Medical Center.

A WALK IN THE MEADOWS

One of my last visits with him. The final family get-together.

It's March 1982. Bright blue sky has pushed in over the region; the winds have dropped. It's warm enough to be out in mere shirtsleeves.

John and Steve have come up from Virginia for the day. Charlie is here. I've arrived in time for lunch, having parked beneath the hickories to the left of the doorway.

My father is dressed in a dark-blue pullover with a turtleneck collar and blue jeans held up by a wide leather belt. He is moving more slowly than he was the last time I'd seen him, just three weeks before—his feet shuffle slightly—but his posture is almost belligerently straight.

"Maybe spring will come early!" I say to him.

We shake hands perfunctorily.

"It's an interlude," he says. "The jet stream hasn't shifted. I can tell just from standing up on top of the rocks."

I picture him standing up there, squinting like one of those Eskimos in old school films.

He tilts his head backward, alluding to the steep jumble of boulders behind the house. *A dare to the forces* . . . Just glancing at that pile of rocks sends shivers down my spine; a geological fault runs close by this ridge, one that I know my father is aware of but chooses to ignore.

"Well," I say, "you've always been good at the weather."

"Come on in," he answers.

Joan is here today. We step out of each other's way in careful silence. Word has reached me through my mother that Joan is "hurt and offended" that I pay her no mind. I snort to think of it, my fantasies savage. I'll pick no quarrel with her if she seeks none with me.

We sit down to lunch. Joan sits immediately to the left of my father. I'm seated on his right. My mother sits next to me. John takes his chair at the opposite end of the table, where he is flanked by Steve and Charlie.

My mother is first to speak. "Isn't this *won*derful?" she says, swinging her smile left and right as if offering her own form of luncheon benediction. Whenever she does this, her neck seems to grow longer.

"Peg!" my father says. He looks at her. "Let's eat."

But my mother is determined. "Why, we should pause to observe our being here together. It isn't every day! . . . I think," she adds, "we should have a toast."

Charlie's face fumbles for a suitable expression. Finally, he grins—the only person willing to acknowledge her mischief.

My mother's undeterred. She has lifted her water goblet. "To the family," she says.

I sit frozen, head down. John raises his glass a couple of inches and gives a faint nod. Steve just eats. Charlie sustains his appreciative grin, his eyes fixed on me.

I expect my father to say, "For Christ's sake, Peg!" It's his ritual rejoinder. Today he merely lifts his right eyebrow slightly and sends a resigned, knowing look down the table toward my mother. "Okay," he says.

Joan has said nothing.

After lunch we congregate in the sunshine outside. On the south side of the house, my father has set out a round glass-topped table and white wrought-iron chairs. The setting affords the full vista—Tuscarora, the whole valley, the remarkable blue of the sky stretching south for thirty miles. As often as I've been here, the sight still staggers me—makes me feel as if I'm flying. At our feet, the rough scree spills steeply down the mountain, littered with broken trees that look like the residue of some recent hurricane. We sit down to drink coffee.

My father talks briefly, matter-of-factly, about his illness. The latest CAT scan shows that the tumor has wrapped around his aorta. It has grown even larger. He can eat almost nothing. When he does, the diarrhea that attacks him is ferocious. Jaundice has begun to gild his skin, even his eyes. He has made the decision to skip further chemotherapy.

"I just don't want," he says, "to climb that mountain again. I'd only to have to come back down the other side." He tells us about a young, aggressive doctor at Hershey who has been putting pressure on him to go back into treatment. He has found the man's insistence very difficult to handle. Aunt Clara, he says, has given him a prescription for the itching the jaundice causes. The itching is a torment.

Both Aunt Clara and Aunt Selma have been here to see him.

He shifts topics on us. "Boys, listen," he begins, and looks around the table at us. "I know that I promised to take a hike with you. But I'm afraid you're going to have to go by yourselves." He gets up. "I've got to rest."

I watch him rise and leave the table. His words are a blade that knifes through me sharply. It is the first time in my memory, perhaps in my lifetime, that my father has forgone an opportunity for a hike.

My eyes follow him the short distance to the house.

Then I turn to my brothers.

"Well . . . ?"

John nods. "Let's go for the walk."

We negotiate the steep drive to the bottom of the hill, then pursue the gravel road that leads out to the far meadows. The crushed shale is unusually firm underfoot for this season.

The four of us are silent. John takes the lead, his long legs setting the pace for the rest of us. Steve walks with him. I hang back with Charlie.

March sun. Wonderful. The air is so clear it's almost purple. But it inspires caution in me. As my father had said about this odd, benign weather, it's a function of the jet stream. Still, the visibility is perfect. The hump of the mountain that lifts to our left is quilled with silver trunks: oaks, mostly, and some hickories. The dark green of the hemlocks marks the undulating course of a stream, and a few slender birches blaze white on the incline. Otherwise the landscape is all muted browns.

We come to a gate. It's the gate that my father had quarreled over with a neighbor. The neighbor had summarily put a heavy padlock on it, cutting off my father's access to the lower part of his tree stands. He and the neighbor had traded tense words (I'd been here to hear them during one of my visits), but my father had won; his steady persistence had simply worn the fellow down. We pass around the gate, whose posts have weathered to a fine, subtle silver, and come abreast of a red barn set back in a field. To the side of the barn, an old harrow shows its rusting discs to the sunlight. It belongs to another neighbor, who lives here only in the summer.

Freed from our silence, we talk nonchalantly about our jobs and various other things. Charlie gets started on the work that he's doing. He has to work very hard and often suffers from the cold.

John asks about my teaching. I inquire about his rug sales. Steve talks briefly about his work in real estate.

We reach the turnaround. It's the point where the meadows and the road give out. The land dips here into forest on three sides. My father's stands of timber lie in a swampy kind of bowl that drops off to our right. Beyond the bowl the land rises, climbing the steep ridge. My mind takes me back to the first time I was out here, only six years ago.

"Well," I say to my brothers, "it looks as if it isn't going to be too long now."

"No, I guess not," John says.

"Have you talked with Dad at all about the mountain place?" I ask.

"No," John says, "I don't know what his thoughts are. I guess Mom is going to have to make up her mind about it once Dad dies, though."

This mobilizes Charlie. For a time he's been silent, but now his whole body comes alive. He wants us, he says, to keep our share of the mountain place; he likes being there, and he's put in a *lot* of work on it with Dad—

We seek to mollify him. I say we understand.

"All of *you* guys have houses of your own!"

He stays belligerent for a minute, then begins apologizing. I tell him it's okay. He's entitled to his feelings.

It's not okay, and all of us know it. I'm sorry that I've even brought the subject up today.

Charlie veers away, his shoulders bent forward and his stride suddenly longer.

I say to myself, *Damn.*

. . .

My mind soon returns to other walks, other meadows. I'd been to McConnellsburg in November, when my father had first learned about some other tests of his. He'd invited Charlie and me to take a long hike with him in a valley west of here, in a state game preserve with a big beaver colony. We'd skirted their dams and watched in vain for a glimpse of them. We'd swung up the hill into a broad quilt of meadows planted with different grains for the wildlife: corn, millet, other grasses. My father described the black bear he'd seen there once, a big, grunting fellow getting fat for the winter. There were raccoons, deer, turkeys.

I'd said to my father, as we tramped through the meadows, how strong he seemed to me. "That's the hell of it," he'd answered. "In a way, I've never been more fit in my life. You know, pancreatic cancer is this chic new cancer they don't understand yet."

"Chic cancer"? Jesus.

But I made no comment.

He spoke about the wood he was cutting every week, still. Cords of it. Cords! In my mind's eye I could see him down there in the hollows, sending the smoky whine and snarl of his chain saw up the slopes. He wasn't going to quit, by God, until he had to.

And on our way to the Alamut: that old man we'd encountered as we reached the last valley, a plunging ravine that had dizzied my sunburned senses. The child on his back he was carrying all the way across the mountains to Tehran like a bundle of firewood . . .

We trudge up the long, twisting drive, breathing deeply. The four of us silent.

My father is back outdoors in his sunglasses, his head tilted up to catch the benefit of the sun. He looks as if he's listening to geological music coming from someplace deep inside the planet.

He's seated at the table. He could easily be a blind man at a sidewalk café.

Joan is sitting with him.

As we approach, she yields to us, moving off toward the house with a hunch of her gaunt shoulders. It's the one—the only—time that I soften toward her and have a quick appreciative sense of her marginal position. Soon enough I close over, mollusklike, hardened again.

My mother is indoors. Charlie sits down for a minute, then lumbers off somewhere. His curtain has fallen; he may not surface again during this visit.

Our talk turns soon to my father's scholarship. The approach of his death has been accompanied by successes: he has recently been out to the University of Chicago to give a series of lectures on his work in metallurgy and the ancient technology of the Mediterranean basin; he has had two books published, one by Yale, *The Coming of the Age of Iron*, co-edited with James Muhly; his articles have been appearing in several major journals.

He's also busy writing, churning out new pieces while he still has time.

I decide to say something that has been on my mind. "It's a shame," I tell my father, "that the academic world has never fully acknowledged you. I can't help thinking you've deserved more recognition."

"I never expected it!" he says. "Dick, I've known for years that the sort of work I do isn't what universities are looking for in their people. Academic institutions want narrow specialists. I just don't fit into any of their niches."

"Still," I say, "it's a shame."

"My rewards will come later. Look how long it took for *The Coming of the Age of Steel* to have any impact. Twenty years!"

"Granted. Still. After all the work you've done—"

My father interrupts me. "I couldn't have worked harder!" I sense that he is offering a kind of summation. "You just can't tally up your life's work in terms of the reception it's been given. If there's anything new in what you say, it'll be rejected. At first. It will at first. And the rejection is *always* going to be superficial. God knows, the good minds can fault some of my scholarship on this detail or that; but that's not what's important. It's the *vision* that's in question. And gradually that vision is going to penetrate the thinking of the really serious people—because they want to *know*. They won't have any vanity. They'll simply set aside their earlier misunderstanding."

His mind shunts sideways.

"You know, it's like these doctors that I've been dealing with at Hershey. They're bright fellows, all of them. This surgeon who did the pair of operations on me—he's a very bright, very alert, very curious doctor. But they've got tunnel vision! Like this young, aggressive doctor I was telling you about: he just can't *understand* why I won't go through chemotherapy again. That stuff put me through the tortures of the damned. And there's no point now! I said to the surgeon last week, after all this bad news, 'You're committed to saving lives. That's what you're all about here. But the time has come now for you to help me learn to *die*.' 'We don't know how to do that,' he'd said to me humbly. 'We don't know how to do that'! So. Now I face extinction."

My father rises.

Unseen fingers have gripped the muscles in my throat.

"By the way," I say to him, my voice slightly hurried, "I really enjoyed your poems."

"Good," he says. He removes his sunglasses. He stands there meditatively while he slips them in their case. His eyes level on me.

He has begun writing verse about the nature of his losses; he has given up playing his violin and viola because his hands no longer work well enough. Never again will he play his beloved Mozart, or Schubert or Haydn, or the Brandenburg Concertos.

One of his poems deals with this subject. As a poem, it's proficient.

"I especially like the way you describe the two cases when you put your instruments away for the last time."

He nods, but I sense that he's ignoring my comment. "I'd like you to take home with you a copy of my article on Cypriot metallurgy. Let me know what you think," he says. "I believe you'll enjoy it."

I promise I will.

The visit is over. My father will talk further with me and my brothers before we make our departures; my mother will scurry out and insist on family pictures, which Joan will take for us with my father's good Leica; we'll have food before we leave; and Charlie will reappear, rumpled and red-eyed, sleepy-looking.

But the visit is over.

My father makes his way back into the house now.

I watch as he goes. His recent loss of weight has been so drastic that his ears flare notably above his shrunken neck and his shoulders have the delicate fragility of an adolescent boy's. His buttocks have wasted to the point that his trousers bag, and his broad leather belt seems to constrict him in the middle.

Joan follows after him. She wears, as she always has whenever I've seen her, a jet-black sweater and black knit pants. Her hair is as black as the opaque shiny lenses of my father's dark glasses. She's so frail and ill that she totters when she walks; it seems as if her ankles could break at any moment.

A coward's impulse seizes me as I watch my father leave us. The aggressive thought hits me—although shame crowds around it—that my father is finally of a size that I could manage. *I could take him now*, I'm thinking. *If he and I fought, by God, I could finally take him.*

I bury this notion quickly.

. . .

At any rate, I've acquired this fresh news from my mother, which she has furtively shared with me during a moment in the kitchen.

Joan's parents have telephoned from Phoenix, Arizona, where they live in retirement, to tell my mother that she ought to give my father a divorce. "He's Joan's husband now," they've said. "You should let him go, Peg. It's what Ted and Joan want."

"Well," my mother has said, "I have no intention of giving Ted a divorce. He's my husband, and I'll keep him. It's none of your darned business!"

"That just shows," they've answered, "how selfish you are."

FINAL ENCOUNTERS

I make two more trips to see him; Marcia joins me for the second. The first is a journey I must make by myself.

The turnpike tugs me west through a land in the grip of a slow winter's ending. My father had been right about that one clear day—it was just an interlude. The weather has reverted to cold, rain, and gloom.

Yet once I've pushed to the far side of Harrisburg, sun sputters through long enough to warm the highway, and in a field to my right, sheep puff up suddenly like mushrooms on the hillside. Miles farther, on my left, a bent elderly couple survey the late March morning, stunned to discover that the world is still out here. The man casts his glance across his sloping front lawn as though assessing flood damage, his grass is so beaten, his shrubbery so gray.

. . .

During this next-to-last visit, the decisive moment occurs at the dining table. We sit, my father and I, in the bright slanting sunlight, which throws a warm bar of gold across our forearms. My mother and Aunt Kay—who has come east to spend a few last days with my father—have discreetly disappeared.

The house hangs upon us like an oversized garment.

At last my father says, "Well, Dick. Here's our chance. If there's anything that you feel that you need to say—"

I shift in my chair. The weight of the moment is not lost on me, and I deliberate on the two long years of separation that followed the disaster we'd had in Jenkintown. My mind lightly grazes the burden of these memories: his having shot Gretta; our quarreling over Joan and her right to this house; his breaking his word that we wouldn't have to endure her that first Thanksgiving . . . But I'm reminded, as well, of Grandma Schultz and Gramdma Wertime—how important it was for me to end well with both of them. I remember Grandma Schultz's waving to me and smiling at me, and this memory resolves me: *Forever is too long to leave things unattended.*

I pause only briefly. As simply as I can, I say to my father, "You made me afraid of you."

My eyes have stayed focused on the table as I've said this. Only once the words are spoken do I find the courage to look up.

My father's face is wrenched. I'm not sure what I've expected, but it is not what I confront now. My father's head has dropped to the side and slightly forward. It's an angle of dejection so profound and moving to me that I look straight at him, absorbed by the sight of him, awaiting what he'll say to me. His lower jaw has lifted and his mouth has puckered slightly, as if a bitter piece of food has just touched his palate.

"It was never my intention," he tells me with anguish, "to make you afraid."

"I believe you," I answer.

I'm suddenly enlightened: enlightened to the fact—no, to the cruel irony of it—that my father has never really grasped his power over others; that he truly cannot fathom his own talent for destruction.

It exists for all that, and I have no inclination to try to absolve him, or to set the past behind me.

Still, I'm ready to accept what he has offered as his answer, and I repeat, "I believe you."

The rest of our talk disappears down a funnel.

The next visit is the last time I see him alive. It's just a week later. Joan is there, and my mother. Marcia. Me. Kay.

And Charlie, too, maybe, but his presence is so fleeting—if indeed he's there at all—that it doesn't register on me.

My father is altered. A single week has ravaged him. His face has drawn inward, his cheekbones jutting outward, his lips parched, collapsing. His skin, and his eyes as well, glow an unearthly yellow from the advance of the jaundice. He is wrapped in a wool shawl atop two sweaters (he's cold all the time now), but the bulk of these garments can't disguise how thin he's gotten. As we talk, one of his hands is fretfully scratching at the other, his fingers small creatures independent of his volition. What hair he has left now has turned completely white. He looks older than ninety.

But it's his eyes that say the most. That fierce deep blue set amid the vivid yellow. His decline is so advanced that his upper right eyelid can no longer open fully, and sags like a sail. I am undone at first by this alteration; it panics me, his losing even this much of his vision. But I don't feel free to say anything about it.

The visit passes in a thin blur of commotion. My mother is cheerful; Kay fills me in on the activities of her children; Joan, in turn, tends to my father's small needs. Marcia is very deft in giving attention to everyone and in trying to leave me space to be here as I need to be. I spend a few minutes wandering vaguely around the house, entirely focused on small things: a pair of sad tulips in a pot in my parents' bedroom (*"Your father hopes to live to see the first tulips blossom—the ones that he planted,"* my mother informs me); the hanging Persian lamps with their copper filigree; the woodstove my father had arranged to have installed in their bedroom . . . And I spend some time staring down into the valley, amazed by how high we sit above it up here.

We convene in the bedroom for the last conversation. My father tires easily; he must rest often.

I'm not exactly sure how the scene comes about, but it unfolds this way: My father is seated in his large upholstered chair. We've all waited in silence while my mother has escorted him back from the bathroom, where his agonies have kept him breathing hard, and occasionally groaning, for some uncomfortable minutes. Once he's settled in his chair, we fan out through the room. My mother has perched herself on the edge of the bed; Marcia sits next to her. Joan stands off to the side, toward the window; Kay is in the doorway, arms folded, smiling wryly. It's just her manner.

The only seat left for me is on the round red hassock that my father props his feet on. "Here. Sit here," he says, and swings his legs away slowly.

I take a seat.

"So," says my father.

I'm the one who must speak now. A fullness is in me. For the next half minute, he and I seem to be the only people on the planet. "It makes me so *sad* to see you suffer," I say to him. "It makes me so sad to see you suffer like this." Each of these syllables hikes my heart farther downward toward some basement in my being; when I get to the bottom, I am pitched forward suddenly, as though a hand at my back has just given me a shove.

I am crying, I discover—*I*, of all people, who almost never cries.

My father reaches forward and gruffly gathers me to him. I hug his waist, he hugs my shoulders. I tell him that I love him. He responds by telling me that he loves me, too.

Then the moment is over and I'm sitting up again, scrubbing tears with my sleeve and trying to steady my breathing.

"Let's have a toast," says my father.

At first no one stirs.

"Come!" he says. "A toast! Peg, go get some glasses."

"But Ted—"

"Just go get *glasses*. Jesus!"

My mother says, explaining, "I just wasn't sure what we were going to toast *with*."

At this my father pauses. "Don't we have some wine or something?"

"I'm not sure," my mother says. "You—"

"Find something," he orders, adding, "Anything will do."

Joan says she has some cold duck in her car.

"Fine," says my father, staring off toward the wall.

I've smiled to myself throughout this whole interchange, comforted, in an odd way, by the familiarity of it.

The cold duck is fetched. Glasses are found. Joan does the honors and opens the bottle. She pours small glassfuls, which are then passed around. I take mine, having handed one to Marcia.

The liquid fizzes softly in the bottom of my glass while my father halts, pondering.

He lifts his glass. "To the family," he begins. I know that, for him, now, this has wider application. For the moment, I accept it.

He continues. "The approach of my death shouldn't grieve anybody. I consider myself to be an entirely fortunate man. I am blessed." He stops briefly. "*If* I've had any mission, it is decently completed; my attention is turned now to those who survive me. My hope for all of you is that you'll find in your lives that . . . that crystallizing center which gives purpose to your actions . . . Yes, and depth to your thinking. Once my spirit has left here, I will search out ways, believe me, of being in touch with you.

"Know," he says, finally, "that I'll be looking down on you with whatever kind of eye the universe might afford me—and wishing you well!"

"Cheers," someone says.

We lift our glasses and sip.

It's my turn, it seems.

I compose my thinking briefly. What is in my mind to say is that we owe to my father, for all the good and ill of it, the opening of doors, of so many doors and windows. In a sense, he has made for us a house of the whole world—has helped us travel, see places, gain knowledge, learn new skills . . . Some of these notions have just occurred to me, and my grip is imperfect.

So when I start to speak, all that comes out is "Thank you." Enunciated in a whisper, my glass feebly lifted.

Silence.

I go on. "You've shown us the way, in so many different things. In so many *rich* things. All of us thank you."

A polite rustling follows.

"Well!" says my father. He bobs his head faintly. Enamored of fine words every bit as much as I am, he has been disappointed that I've failed to deliver anything more than this. Soon the gathering dissolves, and he, Marcia, and I are left to offer good-byes. Marcia counsels him to take good care of himself, her special emphasis on "good." Then she kisses him and slips out of the room, nodding to me. I nod back at her.

When the room has emptied of all but the two of us, I say to my father, "I'm sorry I couldn't summon better words for you." I tell him it was an elegant—and eloquent—toast he'd given.

"That's all right, Dick," he says, and I understand he means it.

"I guess your words daunted me." This admission of mine made, we briefly talk of other things.

Then I say, "I owe you something—the manuscript you've given me. I'll read it soon. I promise."

"I'll appreciate your comments," he says to me plainly.

For how many weeks have I held on to it now?

"Well," I say. I stand there loosely.

"Go!" he says. "Go now!"

I obey, unprotesting. He's exhausted, very clearly. He has closed both eyes now and let his head drift back against the upholstery of his chair. I walk to the door, where I turn and look at him. But there is something not yet finished.

"Dad!" I say to him.

I've weighed if I'll be bold enough to ask this or not and decided that I will be. "Dad. Look at me."

His eyes open slowly. Though his right eye is veiled by the cowl of his drooping lid, his eyes are keen and fiercely blue, set like turquoise in gold. I drink from them quickly.

I say something vague, vague and inane, like *Take care of yourself.* His eyes close again.

Then we are gone.

All the way back to Jenkintown, my wife there beside me, I pilot through a landscape that seems somehow altered. *My God*, I keep saying. The innermost part of my mind turns it over. *My God.* My head's a blank, and everything seems surreal.

My God, I say again. And once more: *My God!*

APRIL WEATHER

It snows. Not during the night, but starting early in the morning on the fifth day of April. It snows noisily and wetly, sheets of it hissing sideways through a sky overturned by the snow's untimely coming. Awakened by the clatter, I throw a curse past the long drapes anchoring our windows, imposing maledictions on the lawn and the street and the parked cars along it, the neighbors' roofs, trees, shrubbery—everything docile and supine enough to accept unobjecting such a vernal affront. "Shit," I proclaim. Oh, shit. Shit. Shit. As though life weren't difficult enough already.

It snows. Keeps snowing. Noon wastes its chances. The afternoon squanders its precious resources.

And still it keeps snowing.

. . .

It lets up at nightfall, by which time a half dozen sodden gray inches have covered everything.

The indignity of cold then arrives to secure them. The thermometer plummets. By nine in the evening, although the sky is still overcast, the temperature has dropped all the way down to 20. I think of the lettuces and onions I've planted, the early spinach. My pea pods.

When I leave for work the next morning, the sidewalk crunches. My raincoat's insufficient; I retreat to the house and discard it in favor of my blue overcoat. I put on galoshes. *Goddamn weather. Goddamn weather.* My fury is idle.

It's April. Snow's fallen.

NO NOURISHMENT

My mother phones to tell me, a day later, that my father has been moved to the hospital in Chambersburg. He's gone there, she tells me, at his own request; it turns out he's been suffering from dehydration during these past days and the itching has grown unbearable, a torment he can't handle. The medication he's been taking is doing no good.

Damn it, I say to myself when I hear this. *Damn you! How could you have let that happen?*

It's unfair, I know.

His final journey, it emerges, has been quite a saga. As might be expected, the snow we've had here in the Philadelphia region, driven by winds, has descended more fiercely on McConnellsburg. The ambulance has struggled to make its way up the drive and succeeded in getting only as far as the sharp bend. The attendants have been forced to fetch my father, carrying a stretcher.

They've had to strap him to it to keep him from sliding. As they've jostled him down the hill, trying not to slip, with my mother walking beside them, the snow has sifted over my father's upturned face. I can picture the bare winter trees careering over him, drunk with sudden motion, as these young men struggle to help him get away to die.

No nourishment, he has said upon arriving in Chambersburg. Fluids, yes; he needs fluids. *But no nourishment. Whatever.*

"He was adamant about it," my mother explains. "The doctor was good, though. He said, 'Okay, Ted.' Your father just doesn't want the agony prolonged."

Good! I'm thinking as I listen to this story. *Good! Give 'em hell! Take your death on your own terms!*

I'm also aware, before the call is even finished, that what I'm really thinking is this: *A temporary setback. He won't die. He's too tough.*

My astonishment at these notions crowds against my realizing that I haven't yet read the manuscript he'd given me. Why am I delaying? What's *wrong* with me, anyhow? My chest constricts on me; I might fail in this promise! Suddenly it seems as if the world's on fast-forward: the manuscript must be read; I must do, I must do—something! . . .

I pull myself back to the present. There's time! For amendment. Right now, if I hurry.

I turn to Marcia and David, telling Marcia what has happened, tincturing the news to make it acceptable to my son.

"Honey," Marcia says. "For heaven's sake! Calm down."

I laugh. I say I'm sorry. I explain that I've promised to read this article of my father's—

"Well, then! Just go do it."

"But I'm so pressed. Jesus."

"*Make* the time! Look. Other things can wait, right now."

. . .

I'm released from a vise. I thank my wife, hug my son, and go up to my study. My father's manuscript, on Cypriot metallurgy, feels cold to my touch, but soon enough I've eased my way into its wealth of information: the island's ancient patterns of deforestation, mining practices, smelting methods, the distribution of ores . . . As I read, I re-experience that odd, antique comfort that my parent knows more than I will ever grasp in a lifetime; that there exist occult formulae and complex equations inscribed in scientific tongues more remote than Aramaic. Pride tugs at me that my father has marshaled such squadrons of data to vanquish his doubters.

It's late when I finish. It occurs to me, irrelevantly, as I set down the manuscript, that my father has missed his hopes to see the year's first tulips. I recall the potted tulips my mother had bought him, whose two pink listless blooms had struggled up from hard soil and were tilting at an angle, as if yearning for sunlight. They craved water, I suspected.

And here, in our borough, the snow has blasted all the forsythia in bloom. Near the Oldsmobile dealer, where a forsythia hedge rims the low fence to the corner, the blossoms are burned; their spring has been wasted. Spring tulips . . . Anyway, I am fortified by the thought that tomorrow I'll fulfill my promise to my father; praise his writing; wish him well; show him again how much I value his intellectual achievements . . .

I go to bed with a sense of having mended some damage, of having propped myself in a corner in such a way that, come morning, I'll know what I face. It's an aggrandizing feeling, infused with solid resolution. I will make good, somehow — even though I'm not sure that they're altogether real — these judgments that I've worked so hard to make of my father's writing. And I intend to be generous.

DEATH

I call the next day to say that I've read the manuscript. I tell him it's one of the best articles he's written. "It moves very well," I say. I go on to tell him that it's commanding, authoritative. I can't, of course, judge the scientific merit of it, but as a reading experience . . .

His voice seems to reach me from an extra-great distance, as if he's pushed a weight toward the vicinity of the phone just to make himself heard.

"Thank you, Dick," he says. "I much appreciate that."

As these tired words reach me, a quick panic hits. I feel I ought to grab my keys and begin the journey westward.

My mother gets on. "Buck, your father can't talk now."

No elaboration.

. . .

I update Marcia. My father is failing. I go about my business, my teaching and department work, numbed by the many miles between me and the scene. I have a restless feeling that there's something I can *do*, that there's some action which, performed in just the right fashion, would undo his suffering, reverse the grim tides that are tugging him seaward. I'm obscurely aware that it's an old family pattern, the talismanic clinging to the magical power of work. So much mental serum is running through my system that I feel almost drugged.

Evening comes. It snows again.

When I call the next day, in the early afternoon, my mother says to me, "I don't think he can talk now."

This is inconceivable to me, that my father can't talk. Of course he can talk! "Put the phone to his ear," I tell her.

She chooses not to quarrel.

A sudden rasping static braids itself into my phone line, and irritation hits me; this is no time for the system not to be cooperating. My brain lurches sideways as I grasp the actual fact. It's my father's voice I hear—no, not his voice. His breathing. An inhuman sound, it's like listening to gravel pour down a rough chute. Except that it pulsates: In. Out. In. Out. A nasal kind of whinny, almost like the sound of an old donkey braying.

"Dad!" I say, lifting my voice to a shout. I must make myself heard over this unwanted static. What do I say? My words are mere nonsense: that his article is fine, that I'm thinking about him, that I want him to, to—I have no idea, in fact, what it is that I say.

"Dick. Hi. John here."

It's my brother on the phone.

He pauses. "Look. It's, ah, getting pretty grim now. We don't think he's conscious."

I think I say something, but he goes on. "Clara's here. She thinks it'll be soon now. She says that *he* has to decide when to let go."

He? HE? Who is *he*? This *he* looms above me like a volcanic mountain, impersonal and cloud-ringed, a fierce force of nature.

"Okay, John," I say when our conversation's finished. "You'll call me right away."

"Yes. Of course."

We both hang up.

It's almost seven-thirty when the phone rings again. I've been out on the front porch staring into the night air, where a full moon hangs in the clear space that rises over our neighbor's shining rooftop.

This time it's my mother. She wears a solemn voice, one edged with weariness, but calm. "Dick your father is dead," she tells me. "He died almost exactly at seven-fifteen."

"Well," I say. A breath escapes me.

It occurs to me to ponder what she has done in the fifteen minutes since my father actually died. Whom has she called first? I wonder. Then it strikes me that my father has been dead for fifteen minutes. A quarter of an hour.

Dead for that long.

I thank her after I tell her that I'll be out first thing tomorrow. I've remembered, too, to offer my condolences to her.

I tell Marcia, then David. "Grandpa Ted has died," I tell him.

"Oh, honey." Marcia hugs me. She says she knows that I loved my father.

"I think," I say vaguely, "I'll go out and walk."

"You go right ahead," she says. Her voice is soft and encouraging.

"Boy!" I say. My lungs lurch.

I laugh.

"Boy." I shake my head.

The moon has milked over in the five or ten minutes since I've last stepped out; the sight of it—glazed, now, by its cataract of cloud—jolts me worse than the news that has sailed over the phone lines. I've expected it, somehow, to be clear and reassuring; that it is not drops the scaffold which holds up my stomach and leaves me feeling that I'm falling through a still, endless space. I say aloud to myself as I start around the block, though I know it is childish, "*The eye of heaven is glazing over.*" I feel betrayed, bereft of solace. I tramp through the snow, repeating the same sentence—"*The eye of heaven is glazing over*"—every now and then glancing up at the sky.

Why couldn't the moon have stayed clear? I wonder. *Just this once. Is that too much to ask?*

I turn to the right when I get to Highland Avenue, then drop down the long hill that escapes Jenkintown, to the bridge over the tracks. I turn again, right, intending to fashion a ragged loop that will lead me to the crest of the parallel hill, a wealthier hill we see from our own high vantage point through the bare wintry trees. I want to get as close as I can to the sky; yet when I reach the angling streets that would take me up the incline, some motion checks my progress and I keep going straight.

My father's words occur to me, words that he had said some months back about dying. We'd been discussing death and common misapprehensions about it. "*Dick!*" he'd said. "*Once you're dead, you're as dead as Aristotle! There's no such thing as a freshly dead person!*" He was right: I hadn't grasped it.

And, I see, I still haven't.

The snow. It has spread like sand over the lawns and the streets, and the sky, too, is sand, a tawny blur in the urban lightness. The moon is tightly wrapped in its cocoon of white threads now; the light it gives is faint and dirty. It's my guess that there might be more snow tomorrow, though it seems to be warming; I take off my gloves and work my hands, closing and opening them. The miracle of life. Lines from *Lear* come to me. *Pray you, undo this button: thank you, sir . . . We that are young . . .*

I don't know exactly what I do when I get home except to begin to get ready for the rest of my life. One thought has played in the back of my mind during my hour-long walk. It has taken root reluctantly and flourished in quiet; grown, grown sturdy; and finally blossomed. I'm almost afraid to admit it to myself. But it's there. Here. No choice is available but to be open and admit it.

Safe now, the thought says. *He's dead at last. It's safe. He's gone.*

You're finally safe.

SIX

THE DAY AFTER

It's just 10 a.m. when I pull into Chambersburg. The interstate has dumped me into the east side of town.

I drop toward the center, past the old Greyhound depot, depressed by the sight of things. The town hasn't really dragged itself awake yet; it lies undisturbed beneath a thin sheet of snow, a light fog muffling its sooty bricks and limestone.

Jesus! Saturday morning. The thought is interrupted by the day's first surprise: right here on Lincoln Way, in front of the old Lutheran church, across the street from an unlit diner, walks my cousin Jay, alone. Thin-jacketed and frail, he looks at first, from the back, like an old man hunched over. But I know it's Jay immediately from the way his ears flare, the curl of his brown hair, his shambling toes-out walk. His head is cocked askance, as if he's listening for messages from some distant planet.

When he fails to notice me, I ease on by. It's unkind of me; he seems so starkly solitary. I've always felt an oddly deep love for my cousin; but the idea of getting entangled with him today, of all days, is one that I dread. Still, I wonder if he knows yet that my father has died.

Soon I am swinging past the grounds of the Falling Spring Church, our family's church for generations, and turning into the drive of the Sellers Funeral Home right next door. Grandma Schultz's death comes back to me at this moment. I recall how my father had met me and my mother here just six weeks ago. It had snowed then, too—was snowing as we arrived—and my father had stopped us on the wide stone stairs. "*Flowers have just arrived here. Peg, did you order flowers?*"

"*Why no, I didn't, Ted. I frankly didn't think about it.*" Her tone had been apologetic.

"*What took you so long?*"

She and I had stopped in a hurry at a roadside stand that was the only thing open and bought a live African violet. It had occurred to neither of us to use the phone to order flowers. My father turned away from us. His skin was a parched red, his face drawn and haggard. In the same cantankerous voice, he said, "*I'll be lying here myself in another six weeks!*"

Six weeks to the day, I think. His guess had been prophetic.

Bob Sellers greets me as I enter the foyer. A brick-faced, genial man built like a fullback, he's too buoyant and hearty for the business of consoling. He guides me inside with his hand on my shoulder, as if he were my coach and I was about to take the mound. Death's friendly partner, he starts a conversation that is anything but gloomy. For years Bob has doubled as the town's weatherman on the local radio station; I had listened to his forecasts in Grandma Wertime's kitchen all through my childhood, and I mention to him now (I can't help bantering) how engrossed Grandma was whenever he came on the air. "*Hush now! Bob's on!"* she'd say. Then came Bob's mellow voice, either threatening hail and thunder or promising deep sunshine.

Bob laughs at this. "Oh, your grandmother!" he says, and draws forth his best smile. "There was never any like her! . . . You know," he goes on, "your dad and I were in school together. In the same grade exactly. I've known your whole family for a very long time."

The room where my father has been set out for viewing is a large curtained chamber with a distinctly churchlike ceiling. Large-leafed palms ornament the four corners. The lighting is muted.

When Grandma Schultz died, she'd been rolled into this room on a large-wheeled gurney, her body wrapped in plastic that the attendants had shoved back from her face, arms, and hands. I'm hoping that my father has been accorded better treatment.

My hope is vindicated. I see at a glance, as I enter the room, that his body has been draped in a series of pleated sheets that resemble scallop shells. He's been suitably presented.

I greet my mother and brothers. "John," I say. "Happy birthday." John is forty-one today.

He gives a rueful laugh. "Well, thank you, Dick," he says.

A shadow snags my eye.

Joan. Joan is here. For the love of holy Christ. She is standing apart, her black hair blending into the room's curtained backdrop. Ripples scale my spine at the very sight of her. My mind does a quick, angered review of the whole history of her involvement with my father. Hurtful words arise in me; I want to say to her—

I force myself away, quelling the impulse to speak.

I turn back to my father. My grandmother's face, six weeks before this, had been a chunk of pale marble scarcely recognizable to me. But my father's, I see as I step toward his body, is unaltered in color; it still wears the bright yellow hue of his jaundice. The changes in him, however, are drastic. To begin with, he's unshaven; a day's full growth has roughened his sunken, wizened face. And death has set a grimace on him. His lips have separated to expose all his teeth, his upper ones especially; the expression this gives him is something of a snarl. And I'm surprised by how cold he is—even colder, it seems, than my grandmother had been—as a consequence of his death and his first long night in refrigeration. The idea of his being packed away in cold storage, beef ready for the shipping, sends indignation through me.

But it's the final alteration that I find so hard to handle, especially on the heels of my casual chat with Bob Sellers. My father, like my grandmother, had donated his eyes. But the taking of them has had a different impact on him. Whereas only a pencil line of blood under my grandmother's right eyelid had betrayed her lack, my father's eye sockets have been stuffed with tissue paper. These huge, empty sockets stare up at me now like those of an ancient Greek statue. My chest, for a second, lurches.

When my senses return, I'm still looking at him, but a glaze has settled on me. I grip his hands lightly, then put my palm to his cheek and brow.

I hope for a thought. None comes. Here I am, in the presence of death for only the second time in my life, and it doesn't frighten me as I'd often thought it might. I speak to my father in a low, absent murmur, memorizing his features, as if there were a chance I could ever forget them. I recall my final glimpse of his now-missing eyes. *"Dad! Dad. Look at me . . ."* The way he'd complied, the blue of his pupils fiercely set in the jaundiced yellow; the way his right eye could open only part of the way.

Put out your eyes! Apologize!

"I AM Picasso!"

I turn away from the fearsome blankness. It's finally too much.

I walk over to my mother. She puts her hand on my shoulder in a gesture of protection that nearly causes me to crack. "Whew!" I say, exhaling. "That tissue paper. Boy—"

"It's rough, isn't it, sweetheart."

"Yeah," I answer, and dig deeper into my throat for the composure I so badly need now.

My eyes land on Joan. I'd entirely forgotten about her while I was tending to my father—had been unmindful of her existence, much less her presence. My anger at her boils back. The black glance I give her says all that it needs to.

We adjourn to lunch at a family-style restaurant just beyond the other side of Route 81. It's a large, bright establishment with huge bay windows that look out over cornfields lightly stubbled with melting snow. The morning fog has deepened, settling in for the day.

The restaurant imitates a hash house out West: redwood paneling wrapped around the large dining room; steer horns mounted on lacquered cedar plaques. Along the stairs to the basement, where the rest rooms are located, the wall is cutely plastered with knicknacks and mottoes. Middle America to the sword's hilt. Country-and-western music leaks obscurely from the walls, lamenting lost loves and thanking God for something or other.

As we dig into our food, I find I'm embarrassed. It doesn't seem right, somehow, our being here like this, our suits and ties on and plenty of money in our pockets. I remember the festive dinners we used to have in my father's absence when he was away on government business; we'd go to Hot Shoppes and splurge, something we almost never did when he was home. We smile now, uncomfortably, at one another and dabble at our carrots. My roast chicken is accompanied by mashed potatoes stiffened with tan-colored gravy and a burgundy slash of cranberry jelly.

My mother fills me in on my father's last hours. The doctor had warned them that just before he died, my father might hemorrhage. They had been spared that. John and Charlie, she said, had been there the whole time, although Charlie had left the room whenever he found he couldn't take it. She and John, however, had stayed right to the end, each holding one of my father's hands. His grip had been like steel, she said. Once he had died, they'd had to pry his fingers open to get their hands out.

"And you say he'd looked up at the moment of his death?"

"Yes," John answers. "It was really quite amazing. His eyes were shut tight during most of the final hours; he didn't seem to be there, though we kept talking to him—you know, giving him encouragement, telling him it was all right. Then, just as he died, he opened his eyes wide and stared *straight up* into the air. As if he could see something. Angels coming. I don't know. And then a single tear, one tear, rolled down his right cheek."

"Remember all the times when we went driving in the country, and Ted's eyes would tear while he was squinting into the distance? Remember how that happened? He'd be wearing those old glasses with the pink, fleshy frames that looked so out-of-date, somehow, and he'd be driving along, absorbed in the countryside and who knows what else, gaze fixed on the roadway and the tears pouring right down the sides of his face along the cracks around his eyes? It never bothered him a bit, his mind'd be off somewhere. Or else he was in a rapture just to be out in the country, driving and driving. I've never seen a man who could be that happy driving, who so much loved the summer, the storms, the orchards, mountains . . ."

I've begun this anecdote in response to John's comments, pulling the muscles of my throat up tight like a sweater in the winter, laughing, recollecting. John, too, laughs . . .

My mother's hand pats mine to get my attention. I come back to the restaurant.

"You know," I say to her, "I passed Jay today. Yep! That's right. Jay Wertime. This morning, just as I was coming into town. On

Lincoln Way East. I wasn't sure if he knew that Ted had died or not. I didn't stop to say hello."

"Oh, I'm sure he does," says my mother. "I called Joe and Vee as soon as I'd called you boys last night." She barely pauses. "How's Marcia?"

"Fine. She was sorry she couldn't come. But with David and all—"

"Please tell her we've missed her," my mother is saying, even before I've finished.

Steve turns to me. He begins to tell me about his latest real-estate venture, then suddenly changes topics and says, "I feel bad."

I ask about what.

"I missed the chance," Steve says. "I missed the chance to see my father one last time. He wanted me to come, and I refused. I missed the chance."

This takes me aback. I say something vague and, I hope, consolatory, about ending with people; but the back of my mind is shouting, Not *"your"* father, goddammit! *OUR* father!

I barely speak to Charlie. When we look at each other, he smiles at me shyly, his lips pursed and working—or else he stares through me toward some far-distant vision that I can scarcely start to fathom. I seem to glimpse my family from beneath a body of water, behold them hovering over me, forms distorted by a ripple. We've agreed to reconvene two weeks from today in order to make plans and to see to arrangements for my father's memorial service. John will call me; I'll call my mother . . .

Suddenly we're departing, spilling outward from some center.

The family heads home, but my business isn't finished. I drive back through town down Lincoln Way East, past the point where I'd seen Jay. I'm almost hoping that I'll see him again, but the family angels have departed and I keep on going till I've reached the town square. I turn left, heading south past the elegant fountain, and make my way toward the steel plant that lies along Route 11. My radar guiding me, I turn right on instinct, anticipating that I'll come to the old railroad tracks. When I see them approaching, my chest gives a small beat of pleasure, and I cross them at exactly that point where, at the age of four, I'd experienced the terror of John's bolting out right in front of a locomotive. I'd stood transfixed while the whole train had passed, endless coal car after coal car, glimpsing John on the far side of the tracks, howling his eyes out. My father had grown ferocious at poor John's expense when the train finally passed. Probably he was as scared as my brother and I were.

I'm looking for my old home: Cardboard Village, that dreary clump of prefabs we had lived in during the war. It's here somewhere on the other side of the tracks, just a few short blocks from the old pretzel factory. For a penny, at the factory, they would give to John and me a whole bag of broken pretzels that we'd eat while walking home. *It must be here somewhere . . .*

And suddenly I find it. The old neighborhood is in the process of being leveled; sharp new condos, made of brick and expensive-looking, are going up in its stead. I pilot my way down a half-bulldozed alley paved in concrete, and know in my bones exactly where I am. I've arrived home. Pine Street! The unit we had lived in has already been demolished, but my sense is unerring: our old street sign still lingers at the corner, its pole smudged with oil, the sign itself rusted. But it still says PINE STREET. I'd last been here with Jay one summer, maybe eighteen years ago, when we were knocking about, having a look at our childhood haunts.

. . . Those empty eye sockets!

Still, I feel anchored, having made this trek back to the old neighborhood. My chest has been refilled, my spirit replenished.

I head on home.

PRESBYTERIAN MINISTRATIONS

We sit, all three of us—John, Steve, and I—in timid, penitential strangeness in a rear room of the church while Falling Spring's rector, a man in his mid-thirties, discusses with us the memorial service we're planning. A heavyish man with a florid complexion and thinning dark hair, he seems as nervous as we are—and yet determined to be at ease; he's in authority here. Relatively new to the church, he hasn't known my father well; but he wants us to know that he hasn't been neglectful. He'd visited Ted in the hospital the day before he died, and he'd traveled out to McConnellsburg to see him ten days earlier.

"Your father," he says, "was willing to recite the Twenty-third Psalm with me the last time I saw him. It gave him comfort, I believe."

This news both does and does not surprise me. My father had known his Bible inside and out, and his embracing an old friend in his time of greatest need hardly strikes me as odd.

At the same time, a sense of unease has slipped its tendrils over me. There's a jockeying going on here, I can see plainly enough, the old Christianizing maneuver that I'm so familiar with from my adolescent days as an Episcopalian convert. I'd fled from the Presbyterians fairly early in my life. We're the lapsed ones, offspring of the more deeply lapsed here, remiss, accountable, finally. I'm irritated by this jockeying because it still has power for me at the same time that I'm wearied by it, this half-reflexive going for the spiritual jugular . . . and over what? I ask myself.

But this rector—his name is Harter—apparently has no such intention; he's too decently motivated; moreover, he's already summed us up: we're a waste of his time, city folk, all of us, out-landers from the territory as well as from his flock. His obligation is less to us than to the larger Wertime clan, and he aims to fol-low through.

". . . So we're agreed," he concludes. "Your father didn't want any 'prayers over him.' But you have no objection to the thoughts I'll share about him, or our doing the Lord's Prayer."

"That's fine," John says. "He, ah, . . .—no, that would be fine."

"And of course there'll be the music. You've made arrange-ments with Phil and Paul."

"Yes."

We're finished, politely dismissed. As we're leaving, the Rev-erend Harter swivels his shoulders toward an idea that, it seems, he must share with us. "Your father," he says—he has stood to his full height now; one of his hands has paused in midair before it drops upon the back of a chair—"was a . . . a quite remarkable man."

The mystery settles on me, as we make our way out, how, early in their lives, many ministers like this (especially those with the thinning hair and overly red complexions) seem to melt pre-maturely as physical beings, their stomachs growing slack and their shoulders getting heavy well before they've hit forty, as if the burdens of spirit they bear are just too much for the body.

You bet he was, I think.

"Boy," I say, smiling, as we step out into the sunshine, "as if we're that obtuse! Jeesh! No wonder Ted fled."

My older brother murmurs, his mouth wrinkling in assent.

I'm thrown back by this April morning, which is struggling toward noon now, on recollections of Falling Spring from the days when I was younger. My father, I recall, had deserted Charlie's christening here in the middle of the service—had simply stood up, walked the length of the nave, and disappeared out the door. We later learned that he'd gone off to chop wood in the mountains, as unrepentant in his defection as it was possible to be. "I've seen plenty of christenings" was his explanation. I was thirteen at the time; Charlie was three already—a child awkwardly old by any sensible Protestant yardstick to be undergoing baptism. What I remember most vividly is how little the family objected to my father's untoward conduct. Ted was simply being Ted; one expected such things from him, and what could one do about it? I also recall how, maybe twenty years ago, an enormous oak had blown over by the edge of the creek, right where it ran through the church cemetery. Among its roots lay exposed the skeletons of a half dozen braves—Potomac Indians, I believe—who'd been buried in a circle in a sitting position; the archaeologists had conjectured that they'd all been killed together in the same fierce skirmish, since the bones gave evidence of wounds on all of them.

Ironically, I'd been christened—John and Steve had, as well—in a fashion even more haphazard than Charlie's. My father's delinquency in matters of religion had resulted in our going unredeemed for a whole decade. The year I turned ten, Grandma Wertime concluded that we risked the pains of hellfire in our ungraced state and summoned the gentle Dr.

Nevius, Falling Spring's longtime rector and true spiritual leader. My cousins Jay and Lynne, and maybe even their sister Kathy, got thrown in for good measure. The bunch of us were lined up in Grandma Wertime's living room and duly sprinkled with holy water while Dr. Nevius murmured something. Lynne, I remember, had shouted in protest, "Hey, that hurts!" and the rest of us had laughed. More than anything, Dr. Nevius had seemed perplexed by the proceedings, as if he couldn't figure out why the matter was so urgent. But my grandmother had sighed an audible sigh of relief once the ministrations were over. I never did understand how her brand of Calvinism had taken such a firm, tenacious hold on her mind.

Maybe it was that old fear of hers—of the family curse.

I blink myself alert from memory, impressed again, as we leave the church grounds, by the huge sycamore that stands right by the iron gate. Lightning had unseamed it when I was eight or nine. Although its fullness was long ago lost to the pruning crews, it still reaches up to a dazzling height and wears its cross-hatched, gaping concrete scar with stubborn courage.

I scan the weather: limping sunlight has given way to slate encroachments. The chill bites through my jacket. We will go back to McConnellsburg now to meet with a forest ranger about the timber on Ted's land, for my mother has the notion that his acres could be a tree farm, a firm investment for all of us that we could draw on in the future.

I wear a headache. Everything is too brilliant for me—the clouds, the patchy sunlight, the bone-white bark higher up on the sycamore. My eyes want shadows.

My father had hated church because he was made to go to it. *"Every year till I went to college, I won a gold star for attendance. I used to win all the Bible-memorizing contests, and once won a showdown to see who could recite the names of the books in the Bible the fastest: Genesis, Exodus, Leviticus, Numbers, Deuteronomy —* "

What will it be like to memorialize him?

Phil Jones and Paul Chalfant have just played the first of their musical selections, a couple of excerpts from Brahms's Opus 122, and the congregation hushes after seconds of commotion. The music still hovers in the air over us, a pair of dusky moth wings made of violin and organ; I'd forgotten how confident Paul was on the fiddle, how sturdy and fine his bowing, though memories still linger of the last time I'd heard him, a snowy night at the mountain place: Schubert's *Death and the Maiden*, Jen on the cello . . . And here is Phil at the organ, that wry smile playing at the edges of his mouth—his way of showing his absorption . . .

So the congregation quiets, and the Reverend William Harter sets forth into his comments on the life of my father. He alone is speaking today. His recitation isn't bloodless—the man has, after all, caught something of my father in his few encounters with him—but his words seek clumsily to climb the stairs toward eloquence. His voice lacks the tenor, the sureness, the vigor that this task requires.

And then it just happens, the event that crowns the morning. Today is an April day of ever-changing weather, and as the service is progressing, dark clouds crowd up against the stained-glass windows, dimming the church's white interior. A wind had joined the music that Paul and Phil had been executing, swishing and rustling beneath the Brahms melody.

Abruptly this wind blows into the church, slugging open a small door on the nave's west side and noisily wrenching its hinges. The jolt of this intrusion is concussive: the rector pauses; the congregation gasps; someone in the nearest pew leaps up and hurries over to try to force the door shut. But the wind presses inward, not to be denied entry, and a second person—my uncle Joe—joins the first, Mr. Freshauer, Grandma Wertime's old neighbor. The two wrestle with the door; Joe reaches up to try to force the hinge to elbow; the door squawks loudly. My aunt Clara is rising to her feet, her back bowed, getting ready to join them, when the wind retreats suddenly. The door eases closed, and Joe and Mr. F. lock it.

The congregation buzzes and a few smiling faces turn inquiringly in our direction. Everybody knows that this incident has meaning.

"Well!" the Reverend Harter murmurs as he gets ready to resume.

The congregation laughs.

Service concluded, we repair to the chapter house that sits on the bank of the Falling Spring Creek for refreshments and conversation. The wind has ebbed, and the sunlight has regained its firm, warm handhold. Spring, it seems, has finally come.

Another surprise—or pair of surprises—awaits me in the course of this family get-together. David is delighted to be around his cousins, whom he sees so rarely, and he and the other children make a boisterous scene of it on the green church lawn. That doesn't surprise me. I'm also not surprised that the family is so warm and welcoming to Kent, the only one of my older children who can be here. What *is* surprising is the friendliness with which Marcia and I are greeted. Many of my relatives haven't seen the two of us either since our wedding or since Grandma Wertime's funeral, which already lies behind us by nearly ten years. Selma's stepson, Ralph, is here, and my father's cousin Milt, all the way from West Virginia. As the afternoon progresses, people mistakenly allude to Grandma Wertime's wedding and to my and Marcia's funeral, and this inadvertent reversal happens often enough to become a standing joke that we all appreciate. No hostility is in it. Marcia and I are welcomed and offered many invitations.

The second surprise is of a more curious nature. I'm in the middle of talking with someone when my aunt P.J. approaches and says, "Come here for a second." P.J., like Uncle Rudy, is a very strict Presbyterian.

How typical of her, I think, to want to be bossy.

I obediently follow her to an uncrowded corner, where she presses a white envelope into my hand. "Here," she says, looking me straight in the eye. "We want you to have this. You and your brothers."

I make a face, say "Okay!" and put the envelope in my pocket. When we get back to Jenkintown later that evening, I'm reminded of its presence as I'm hanging up my jacket. I take it out and look at it. The envelope is plain, about the size of paper money, and the single word "Dick" is inscribed on its face in P.J.'s dark, slanting hand. What *is* this, I wonder? When I open it, I discover that it contains canceled checks that Grandma Wertime had written me, checks stretching back, as I see from the dates, to my undergraduate days. There are maybe fifteen of them.

"What the—?" I murmur aloud to myself. "Jesus," I say to Marcia. "Look at what P.J. has given me."

Marcia frowns, as puzzled as I am. "Is it some kind of joke?"

"How the hell would I know?" I exhale hotly. "What a quirky thing to do—and today of all days!" I'm upset enough to call John long-distance, but he's as much in the dark about these checks as I am. He's been given his, too. I call P.J., finally, confess that I'm perplexed, and ask her to explain.

"Why, they're souvenirs!" she tells me, puzzled that I'm puzzled. "I was cleaning out all of Grandma's old papers and thought that you, John, and Steve would want to have them. You can keep them as mementos!"

I am reminded, once again, of the reasons I've kept myself distant from the family for so long, have held myself on my urban perch looking out toward the rural landscape.

But my thought goes no further.

My mind returns, instead, to the door slamming open; the riot that followed; the whimsical comments made to me and my brothers.

And yet I feel I know better, better than all the others do as I prepare for bed this evening, what was being communicated by the wind in the church there; for it was in my presence that my father had spoken about his looking down on us, about accepting whatever eye the universe afforded him . . .

I will raise the devil with you under any circumstances! I inhabit all the winds now, ride the sunlight, the tornadoes; I can fall as snow upon you, and will jolt your doors open. I AM the power of the weather!

. . . Well, hell, not really.

I'm succumbing to simplicities as I grow sleepy . . . And yet the thought sticks with me: My father had chosen to commemorate himself.

EPILOGUE: STORM

How swiftly a life ends! A second memorial service takes place for my father two months after the first, at the Smithsonian Institution. In attendance, together with many members of the family, are my father's friends and colleagues—government officials, some of whom go back to the OSS days and the State Department years. Several people speak: Joe Yager; Dick Arndt; Larry Wallace, who works for the Justice Department; Ezat Negahban; Joy MacFadyen Bulluck from the USIA; Cyril Stanley Smith, down from MIT . . . And I end the service by reciting a poem, Tennyson's "Ulysses," which captures me so wholly while I'm busy speaking it that I find myself transported to a wave-smashed embankment—

> *The lights begin to twinkle from the rocks;*
> *The long day wanes: the slow moon climbs: the deep*
> *Moans round with many voices. Come, my friends . . .*

The fate of the house, then, after my father's death: My mother, eager to unload the place, puts it on the market—wants out of it quickly, at almost any cost. Unbeknownst to my mother, Joan succeeds in acquiring it the following October, through the use of a front man. The family is well rid of Joan. Her flurry of demands, strident phone calls, and threatening letters has wearied the whole clan during the weeks my father lay dying and in the immediate aftermath of his death. In another six years she'll be dead herself, of cancer—claiming to the end (so we'll hear from people who live on the mountain) that the house has killed both of them, her and my father, such a strange mix of chemicals had gone into its making . . .

And the dogs, the hapless dogs. Two of them remain at the house after my father's death in April, black Bert and tan Leo. Having shot Gretta, my father had considered shooting them as well, but never got around to it. My mother is distracted by her efforts to decamp and leaves Bert and Leo very much to their own devices. Summer comes; she moves. The next winter proves bitter. One cold afternoon sometime in February, Charlie and my son Kent drive up to the place. Joan is now owner, but she hasn't moved in yet. My brother and my son find the two dogs on the mountain. Their emaciated bodies lie several feet apart, frozen and grizzled; snow covers both of them. Charlie, murmuring softly, drops to his knee by the nearest of the two and carefully dusts the snow from it. It's Bert, the gentle black one. He takes a long minute to stroke Bert's stiff fur.

The final visit I pay to the house is a visionary one. While purely imagined, it has become so real for me that, all these years later, I couldn't claim it didn't happen . . .

The key fits stiffly in the new front-door lock that my mother has installed as a sensible precaution. I turn the knob and push, but meet such resistance that I have to set my shoulder to the door to shove it open. It answers with the harsh metallic shriek of swollen wood. It's a humid summer day.

I step inside. An empty house on a mountain is an open invitation; I have no inclination to get blindsided, not by insects or animals. Or people, for that matter.

How strange the place feels! It's been just three months since I was in here last, a scant three months since we did the big cleanout and a little over four since my father's death in April. This is the third week of August. It feels like a decade.

The house is just a shell now, a large booming cavern that catches quick echoes and magnifies my footfalls. Workmen have been in here to take down the fixtures and rip up the carpeting, all to be replaced before the house can be sold. The cracked concrete flooring is damp and grim; a dank prison odor, a deep, sour scent of the kind you encounter in old European dungeons, fills the whole place. Mouse droppings and the dusty winged debris of dead insects litter the concrete. It looks to me, too, as if the birds have gotten in here; small clots of feathers sit on some of the windowsills, and bird dung stains one corner of the living room.

I ought to open some windows and air the place out. But there are thunderstorms coming, and anyway the humidity is even worse outside. Besides, I'm not intending to stay here for long. I've made the trip out here as a favor to my mother, just to check on the place. To be sure that no faucets or toilets are leaking and no extra lights are on. So far we've been lucky that there's been no vandalism.

In the kitchen, on one of the counters, I find a rusty nail. At first it seems like an ordinary nail, but when I pick it up and look at it, I realize it isn't: it's a square, hand-forged nail of the kind that was used in colonial times. It still bears the marks of the blacksmith's hammer, the crescentlike dents where it was pounded into shape. The rust's superficial, a fine red powder that comes off on my hand. When I tap the nail against the counter—it's still surprisingly heavy—it gives a sturdy ring. Who put it here, I wonder? . . .

It's possible that my father has sneaked in here since his death and left it as a token of his enduring concern.

How hard he'd worked to become a scholar! So dogged; so determined. When I was a boy, he'd skip lunch every day to go to the Library of Congress to do research for an hour. On getting home, he'd sit down at a messy old desk tucked away in my parents' bedroom; it was piled high with note cards, with photos of African tribesmen smelting iron ore in small furnaces buried in the ground. Books. Maps. Articles. The stuff he had was endless. He was tough enough to live with even when he was busy working. He'd want the house quiet—this with four growing boys—and would growl or bark at us if we interrupted him.

But there were other sides to him—his music; his love of sports; the hikes and all the outings he used to take us on. He became, in his own way, a kind of "neighborhood father" in his willingness to include other kids in our activities. On soft summer nights he'd read aloud to us. There'd be a tap at our back door; a clump of neighborhood children would be standing by the screen. "Is Mr. Wertime going to read tonight?" The question was asked shyly. If the answer was yes, my father would appear, his hair brushed, khaki shorts on, a fresh white T-shirt over his broad, tanned chest.

In minutes we children would be sprawled on the floor or propped against the stairs in our modest living room. Maggie and her brother; Lynne and Diane; Butch Sheels and his sister; the Waters girls, maybe. Skinny legs drawn up to serve as shelves for chins.

My father might be reading *The Adventures of Huckleberry Finn* or some other favorite—*A Connecticut Yankee in King Arthur's Court*, Thomas Bailey Aldrich's *The Story of a Bad Boy*. It made little difference. When my father started reading, we were carried away, all of us (John, Steve, and I would find our places on the floor, in among the other bodies), to the farthest shoals of being, to the stark cold waters of the raging North Atlantic or to silly hippo antics on the Limpopo River. We'd be transported into caves where bats swirled darkly or buried treasure lurked, and guided back out again to a distant windy plain where Achilles meditated on his great rival, Hector. My father's brilliance as a reader consisted in his investing every voice, every sentence, every heroic action, every heartache and injustice, with a *closeness*, a passion, that would cause the living room to fall away from all of us and bring us to the scene where the action was unfolding. We became, as we listened, a band, a small tribe, suspended in a sleep: a communal gathering of wishes that our touching, longing bodies communicated to one another. For the moment, we were held.

I walk from the kitchen into the big living area. This might not be the best of days for me to have come up here. Dark clouds have already pushed into the valley, gray ragged jellyfish moving with the currents. My father must have watched storms like this approaching during his childhood summers at the old family farm in the hills above Wheeling—storms that boiled up in the Ohio River Valley and rolled across the country with a threatening commotion. After his father died and his grandfather, Grandpap, put him to milking the family cows, he must have dreamed sky-big dreams, must have started to build the vision that carried him out to the Alamut, and then to this mountaintop. A dream of revolution . . .

During the early years of their marriage, my father told my mother several things about himself: that he intended to sleep with eighty women before he died; that it was the war—the Second World War—that had made him so brutal; and that at heart he was little more than "an insecure farm boy," having spent all those summers on the family farm near Wheeling.

He also told her that we—his sons—should not defend our-selves if he decided to beat us; that being a trained killer, he might lose his temper and murder one of us.

So my mother admonished us throughout our childhood, whenever it appeared that we were about to get a thrashing: "Now, don't fight with your father! It might get him angry. You know he could kill you!"

I believed her. And him.

I've loitered too long. There's the downstairs to check. The window locks. The toilets. The faucets. The power. We leave a bulb burning on each of the floors to discourage intruders, though we know it's just a token. Like the mountain place, two valleys over, the house is sufficiently out-of-the-way that maraud-ers could do damage and no one would know it.

Storms develop fast here. Along the crown of Tuscarora, dense black thunderclouds have set up their tents. Flashes of lightning are exploding from this dark force, shaking the farmlands. I'd hoped to clear out before the big storm descended, but I've moved too slowly. Had I started a bit earlier, I might have crossed Tuscarora and taken refuge at the mountain place.

That can't happen now. The rain has crossed the valley, a grim sheet of canvas; it has raced toward this ridge and swiftly climbed the rocky slope. I stand and watch it come. The first drops sting the big plate-glass windows with a sharp sound, like hail. I wish that I had at least a chair to sit on; I've always feared lightning, and thunder—loud thunder—drops a trapdoor beneath me.

This isn't just a storm; it's a late-summer storm. We're pushing at the margins of hurricane season. The winds have escalated into a harsh, steady keening. At first they'd whipped themselves in periodic spasms; now the gusts rising from the trough of the valley make the loud rush of rain sound as if it's falling *upward*. The rain hits so heavily against the big windows that the house feels like an ark being tossed by rough seas.

The first bolt of lightning hits nearby, with a *whang!* In an old, fearful reflex, I drop to a crouch. For a second the floor wobbles. A second, harder *whang!* hits even closer, with a sharp rifle crack, and an earthshaking tremor runs across the damp floor. *Oh Christ!* I murmur. I fight an old impulse to run and hide somewhere, a dark closet maybe—anywhere I won't see these white flashes.

But I regain my reason and pull myself upright. My breath rasps hard against the walls of my lungs, and my heart bangs wildly. There's nowhere to flee to.

A new sound penetrates my senses at this moment, a muffled pinging noise, like the trickle of water. It is: an actual trickle. My gaze soars upward, along the barrel-vaulted ceiling. The roof, I see, is leaking around the solar panels, whose faint rectangular outlines are ghosting into view as the leaking continues. Slim, dark fingers of water push through, but they don't drip down directly; they slide along the ceiling, dropping lightly to the floor about a foot from the wall. When they hit, they dance with a tiny bounce before they settle.

This dripping makes a murmur, a murmur distinct from the loud rush and howling of the storm outside, which has grown so in malice that trees barely visible at the bottom of the rock slope are whipping and lashing their tops like switches. The separate sounds seem to play on two different channels, as though I have two kinds of hearing, one for each form of noise.

Listening to the trickle, I have an odd vision. The storm abates; the winds subside; the seas roll back; the trees stand upright to shake fat droplets onto the rocks and forest cover. Inside the house, however, the trickle increases. It swells to music of the kind made by mountain brooks early in the spring when the winter snows are melting. Bird voices join it, the calls and chirps and twitters heard in brightening morning hours as the summer solstice nears.

And, as all this is happening, green shoots begin to push up through the concrete, right where I'm standing: ferns and soft mosses, the tendrils of vine growth. Sassafras saplings and the broad-leafing ailanthus unfurl about me. Trees spread their branches. Bright orchids bloom. The birds grow louder. The house is transforming itself into a jungle—all while the trickle of the rain from the high roof murmurs and murmurs. It's a symphony of noises . . . that occurs nowhere but inside my own head.

ACKNOWLEDGMENTS

Thanks are due to many people. They include my family at large, a host of whose members have been very helpful in giving me information as well as support and encouragement, my mother in particular; her patience with my questions has been extraordinary. To the following former members of the government community I owe thanks for interviews: Phil Jones, Joe Yager, Ed Fried, Abe Sirkin, Peggy and David Nalle, Joy MacFadyen Bulluck, David Larsen, and Walt Rostow. For help with the geology of the Appalachian Mountains, I thank Professor Maria Luisa Crawford of Bryn Mawr College. I am grateful to Bob Scott for helping me understand how my father built his house and for other useful details. For reading portions of earlier drafts of this book, I owe special thanks to Marcia Wertime, Jeanne Foster, David Bassuk, Rupert Thomson, and Tobias Wolff. Tobias Wolff's timely help was instrumental in moving this book toward publication. To Michele, Kent, David, and Geoffrey—my four children—go my love and gratitude for their sustained support. My agent, Amanda Urban, has championed this book with heartening effectiveness; and Jonathan Galassi, together with his editorial staff, has made publishing this book with Farrar, Straus and Giroux a wonderful experience. I thank, as well, Deena Adler, whose sustained wisdom has strengthened me. My deepest debt of all is to Alan Williamson, without whose friendship, keen critical eye, and unending support this book might never have been completed.